Grass Seed in June

The Making of an Architectural Historian

JOHN MARTIN ROBINSON

with a foreword by
SALLY BROWN

MICHAEL RUSSELL

FOR

HUGH MASSINGBERD

First published in Great Britain 2006
by Michael Russell (Publishing) Ltd
Wilby Hall, Wilby, Norwich NR16 2JP

Typeset in Sabon by Waveney Typesetters
Wymondham, Norfolk
Printed and bound in Great Britain
by Biddles Ltd, King's Lynn, Norfolk

Contents

Foreword

'O happy Browns and Robinsons!' John Betjeman, *Summoned by Bells*. The Browns first heard the Robinson memoirs on a chilly evening in May 2004 when we were staying with John in his handsome house at Barbon. To hear the memoirs read by the memoirist is, of course, ideal. All through that evening – and the next, when we demanded more – we listened to John, his clear and distinctive voice swooping up and down as he impersonated different characters and added emphasis to particular passages. One sentence struck me particularly. He described the Vespers chants on Sunday evenings at Fort Augustus, his Benedictine monastery school in the Scottish Highlands, as 'one of the beauties of life, like grass seed in June', which always brought tears to his eyes. It sounded faintly familiar, as perfectly coined phrases often do. I suggested it would make a good title for the book.

The 'private world' of his idyllic early childhood days is beautifully evoked and his powers of memory are extraordinary. His earliest recollections, of a white marble lion ('a reduced copy of that on the staircase at Caserta', as the pedagogic adult voice explains) a lookout tower and an ancient stone bath, set the elegiac tone and whet the reader's appetite for what is to follow. His antiquarian's love of fact and detail and his sudden dramatic pronouncements ('I drank alcohol from infancy') strongly conjure up his presence. The story told here is by turns fascinating, hilarious, melancholy – even, at times, horrific. 'Other people's genealogy is a terrible bore,' John writes – but he weaves his own into an engaging story, peppered with surprising observations: 'Most English family trees are egg-shaped.' The litany of family names – Aloysius, Ignatius – helps to conjure up the Catholic past, and we sympathise with the author's occasional shrieks of horrified disdain ('artificial ski slope and leisurama' replacing an ancestor's millstone quarry). 'Let other pens dwell on guilt and misery' wrote Jane

[7]

Austen – not a suggestion taken up by this author as he begins to describe his school life at Fort Augustus, an 'austere, cold, cruel place', which he sums up as 'Gordonstoun with God'. This section arouses strong, occasionally alarming feelings in the reader. Surveying the emotional and academic damage he suffered during these years, John declares 'It took me decades to recover.' There is some light amidst the gloom, however. He admits that eventually 'I found the parts which suited me': the 'true tradition' of the place, the landscape, the libraries, the Latin liturgy. In contrast, the University of St Andrews is 'a medieval dream', with good music and sympathetic spirits. Here, at last, he is 'a square peg in a square hole', with a burgeoning social life, spending long, delightful summers with friends in Italy.

In 1970, a research student at Oxford, he finds the city 'a kind of English architectural nirvana', into which he 'fits like a glove' – emphasising his 'passing resemblance to the young Swinburne' by growing a little red beard and wearing black. (This was when I first met him, happily exchanging *bons mots* over coffee with his dazzling friend Colin McMordie.) A perfect sentence sums up his feelings at this time: 'Looking from the windows of the Codrington Library towards the dome of the Radcliffe Camera you could almost imagine yourself in a princely Baroque abbey somewhere in the Holy Roman Empire.' The young man who had been 'hopeless at maths, science, rugger and soldiers' is on the cusp of a new and rewarding life, eventually leading to London, that 'admirable organisation' the GLC Historic Buildings Division and a distinguished career as one of the leading architectural historians of his day.

British Library, September 2006   SALLY BROWN

I

The Marble Lion

I have never lived anywhere commonplace. From earliest childhood in Lancashire, there have always been architecturally interesting surroundings. Do carts come before horses? Was my passion
for buildings a product or a cause? We left Whittle Springs when I
was seven and I have never been back, but my babyish memories of
this derelict spa are of an astonishing place. Was it a fantasy? A
white marble lion stood in the long grass, a reduced copy of that on
the staircase at Caserta. I used to ride on his back and feed him with
sticks and leaves. There was a lookout tower, a domed rotunda we
called the 'Monkey House', an empty Swiss cottage lodge, a large
rectangular stone-lined outdoor bath, which went down to
Australia, so we believed, and a 'Tudor' hotel, the Howard Arms.
All were embedded in jungle. An overgrown kitchen garden was a
tangled thicket of unpruned apple trees and giant blackcurrants
through which we tunnelled and in the heart of which we built a
secret den. This was my private world where my sister Anne and a
few neighbouring children, Southworths, Walmesleys and Billing-
tons (all good Lancashire names), our black cocker spaniel Whisky,
and other friends ran wild.

Only the scale is exaggerated by childish memory. It all existed
more or less as recalled. The lion, which seemed as big as that at the
south end of Westminster Bridge, was only two feet high, and the
currant trees were just old bushes. The extraordinary buildings,
however, were real. Many years later, leafing through Charles
Hardwick's *History of the Borough of Preston and Its Environs*
(1857), I came across an engraving showing sprucely laid out
grounds with winding paths and the familiar buildings. The whole
place had been laid out by the Standish family as a short-lived spa
and pleasure garden in the early 1840s, with a chalybeate bath and

Whittle Springs. From Hardwick's History ... of Preston.

'famed alkaline fountains', becoming a popular destination for horse-drawn charabanc parties, but later falling into ruin and decay. It was thought to have been on the site of a Roman bath, and Roman coins had been discovered in the nineteenth century. Hardwick's description in 1857 gives a good impression:

> The neighbourhood of the Springs has been converted into beautiful pleasure grounds, and a commodious hotel erected with baths and other conveniences. The scenery of the district is varied in its character and extremely picturesque. From some of the neighbouring eminences, a large portion of the Lancashire coast is visible... The alkaline water is spoken of, and has been compared to that at Baden Baden.

Our house in a Jacobethan mullioned and gabled range stood on the northern edge. It had been divided into three houses with 'ours' in the middle. I have no memory of who occupied the east end. In the west end lived the Hodgkinsons, two white-haired sisters and their surviving bachelor brother who all lived together. The sisters were widows. Their young men had both been killed in the First World War, so had their other brother, and his framed death certificate with George V's arms hung on the wall. The sisters had never remarried and never referred to the war. Their house was untouched Victorian, gleaming and clean (unlike our own). I loved to browse in the little-used 'front room' with its china in glass cases. The two old ladies were very kind to me; perhaps they saw my sister and me as the children they never had, as they lost their husbands so soon. They used to give us 'currant wine' when we visited which we called 'cough medicine'. I drank alcohol from infancy. I would start coughing as soon as I was through the door and the bottle would be produced and those small port-like glasses (which nobody uses now). They were not at all fazed by a little boy precociously interested in old china rather than football, and I have some pretty white and gold coffee cups of unusual shape which I admired and which they let me have. I suspect that these cups may have been a wedding present, but they never said. One of the sisters was later knocked down and killed by a careless motorist while walking home from church, but we had moved away by then.

Our cocker spaniel Whisky was killed on the same road. He was greedy and used to run off to the Catholic primary school at South Hill where the generous 'dinner ladies' gave him the leftovers. He then waddled home, but one afternoon he was not swift enough and was run over by a lorry near the Red Lion pub. We wept but were left with a memorial: his little paw mark in the kitchen floor where he had run over a patch of wet cement, much to the builders' annoyance. Whisky was in due course replaced with a black labrador called Raff; she was so gentle-mouthed and such a good retriever that she was able to drop live voles or mice into our outstretched hands.

There was nothing grand about Whittle Springs. Our part was quite small with a sitting room and dining room, modern kitchen and old cellars, bedrooms and a bathroom. It had been bought by my grandmother specially for my parents when they married in 1947, after the war. My parents were probably luckier and more comfortable than many young couples in those austere years, but it was no idyll. My grandmother's 'generosity' was provisional, and my mother never liked Lancashire. She gave up on this little house almost immediately. That may have been partly my fault. I was her first child and my birth, I was told, was so horrendous that she was left anaemic and lacking in energy for years after.

My father who was handy and good at art had tried to make the house pretty – marbleizing the chimneypiece in the sitting room, graining the woodwork in the dining room, and furnishing the rooms with some of my great-grandparents' things, including an eighteenth-century oak wainscot chest which had been rescued from a farmer who stored cattle food in it, and all of which I now have. But, always childlike himself, my father soon gave up on the minutiae of domestic life and spent his free weekends shooting on the Moss at Catcrag, fishing at Lunesbridge (properties in Westmorland belonging to my grandfather), or going to motor races at Oulton Park with his friends. He was mad about cars. As I can first remember the house – perhaps only four years after their moving in – the place was already a wreck, the grass unmown, the paint peeling, uncleared gutters overflowing and leaving green damp stains down the walls. It was bliss.

We children used the drawing room as our playroom, running round on the furniture without touching the floor, blacking our faces with soot from the fireplace, wrapping ourselves in the curtains. Eventually my grandmother, appalled, took all the better furniture away saying she had only 'lent' it, not 'given' it to the newly married couple.

The atmosphere at home was often unhappy, though both our parents loved us. It might have been easier if they had not, and everything had been less complicated and unconventional. My mother was different. She was not a cradle Catholic, she was not a Northerner. Her father had been born in London and later settled in South Africa. When I was young my mother's family, the Adams and Coopers – grandparents, two uncles, one aunt and all my first cousins – lived in Cape Town, far, far away on the other side of the world. My Adams grandparents came over some years for Christmas, in a flurry of excitement, on the Union Castle Line, bringing huge red and green cellophane-wrapped baskets of fruit, sweets and the rich cousins' cast off clothes for us impoverished ragamuffins to wear; rationing and shortages were still part of daily existence in Attlee's Britain, and into the 1950s.

My mother's family were Scottish Lowlands in origin come down to East Anglia as farmers, like many others during the Agricultural Revolution. They had no money until my uncle made a large fortune from boat-building, recycling metal for Japanese industry and property development in Cape Town. But *her* family did not count. They were Protestants. They did not own land. When 'Family' was mentioned (as it frequently was), it was my father's family, the Robinsons and the Cottons, who were meant, though they were not particularly interesting. But we lived in their shade, surrounded by their old furniture and their property in various stages of dereliction. My grandmother was a Cotton and my father was named after his uncle, John Cotton, who, after starting to study for the priesthood at Ushaw, was killed at sea on HMS *Simoon* in 1917. My grandmother, who worshipped her brother, kept his cricket bat and gold half-hunter watch and eventually gave them to me. I have never used the bat and have always hated cricket.

Other people's genealogy is a terrible bore, though it can have its funny side. The smart Edwardian architect Philip Tilden, who entitled his memoirs somewhat tendentiously *True Remembrances*, goes on for pages about his Kentish yeoman ancestors, the scent of hops, the rosy brick farmhouses, the rich tilth of the fields, and does not mention anywhere that he was born in Birmingham. I was born in Preston.

My family was an industrial or mercantile family, descended from minor gentry. One of my great-grandfathers had owned the quarries at Whittle Hills, near where we lived, the other a wholesale cotton warehouse in Preston, while my great-great-uncle founded an iron works in Birmingham – the Victoria Ironworks which made bedsteads and munitions. Other cousins had Lancashire cotton

mills. The Robinsons were originally Protestant weavers who went
to Ireland after the Battle of the Boyne. My great-great-great-great-
great-grandfather Henry I settled as a handloom weaver in Co.
West Meath in the reign of Queen Anne. The textile industry in the
early-eighteenth century was spread through the Irish midlands as
well as Ulster, where it concentrated later. Henry I prospered, and
he and his son Samuel invested modestly in land – acquiring a
couple of hundred acres. In the 1760s Henry the Weaver's son,
Samuel of Ballykilroe House, stopped calling himself a weaver and
described himself as a 'gentleman' in the marriage settlement
(1764) of his son, Henry II, to Esther, daughter of Thomas Coates,
'gent', from Co. Longford. This rise in the world was not too dizzy
or prolonged. Their eldest son, Samuel II, married Miss Matthews
of Mount Mellick, Queen's County. His younger brother Henry III,
also a 'gent', had a son Henry IV. My great-great-grandfather.

Henry IV was born in 1807 and returned to Lancashire, then
about the most economically buoyant place in the world, on his
twenty-first birthday in 1828 to seek his own way. He set up business in Friargate, Preston, as a 'general dealer', selling buckets and
small agricultural bits and pieces, at one stage also describing
himself as a 'toy dealer'. Seven years later, after he had accumulated
a bit of capital, he married Ellen Rainford from Whittle-le-Woods.
Her family were small tenant farmers and recusant Catholics, who
introduced, as well as Catholicism, a long-lived gene. Many Rain-
fords lived into their nineties or even to be a hundred, when few
people did. Henry and Ellen had six children. Most English family
trees are egg-shaped.

Their eldest son, William, was educated at Stonyhurst and lived
at Blackbrook Hall, a small Georgian house at Hoghton near
Preston. He developed the business into manufacturing, eventually
moving it to Birmingham where he established the Victoria Iron
Works at Deritend (which was eventually sold in 1920). He
married another Catholic Lancashire lass, Ellen Pope (of the same
tribe as the poet Alexander Pope, who was of course a crypto-
Catholic), from Fernyhalgh near Preston, famous for its old Marian

shrine in the fields. He 'relapsed' to Anglicanism however: in his will he left money to the Royal Shakespeare Theatre at Stratford, to hospitals and schools, but emphatically not to any religious charity. Both his sons were brought up as Protestants and educated at Bedford School. Neither married and when the younger, an eccentric itinerant bachelor, died he left my grandfather Joseph enough money to buy Catcrag Farm, Nichols Moss and some woodland at Witherslack in Westmorland and a smaller farm, and a bit of the River Lune at Lunesbridge near Tebay, also in Westmorland; places where my father was to spend many happy days with gun and rod. Together with my great-grandfather's purchases these properties gave me a complacent feeling of being 'landed,' which some found tiresome.

I once childishly sing-sang to the spirited daughter of a neighbour: 'My grandfather's a landlord.' 'I couldn't care if he's a pig' she replied. When Great-Great-Uncle Henry moved his part of the business to Birmingham, my great-grandfather – Aloysius (their youngest brother who died of TB as a youth was called Ignatius) – kept the Preston warehouse going and made it into a wholesale cotton business ('J. & A. Robinson Ltd. Founded 1828') with shirt manufacturing, hosiery and 'Hoghton Tower Brands'. He also acquired land in the Fylde and at Whittle-le-Woods. He had other business interests, in addition to the warehouse. In 1896 he bought an outlying part of the Talbot-Clifton's land on the edge of Blackpool and developed it as the 'Bloomfield Estate' with shiny pimento red brick shops and terraced houses along Central Drive and Bloomfield Road. My family have now owned this increasingly grotty property for four generations. It is today a blight of 'chippies', Indian newsagents, purveyors of UPVC double-glazing and DHSS tenants. At least they (sometimes) pay the rent. But not exactly a blue chip investment. One has hoped in vain that it might become a 'development opportunity' and the embarrassment of it might be gilded away.

The other side of my father's family, the Cottons, were also beneficiaries of the Industrial Revolution and were the reason why we lived at Whittle-le-Woods. Unlike the Robinsons, they were a good-looking tribe. My grandmother who was not exactly a snob – far from it – liked a little romantic exaggeration. Thus a cousin who served as a captain in the Army in the First World War was always referred to as 'the Colonel' (at least he was awarded the MC), and another relation who was Vicar-General of Denver, Colorado was called a 'bishop'. Her cousin Dr John Cotton was assumed to be 'President' of Ushaw (the Catholic seminary near Durham) – he was in fact the Junior Prefect of Studies there. She said that her great-great-great-grandfather John (born in 1757) was the youngest son of Sir Robert Salusbury Cotton of Combermere Abbey in Cheshire. He, Peter Todd and John Horrocks had all met as young men and come to our part of Lancashire, after the construction of the Leeds–Liverpool Canal (1770s) and its Preston branch, built by the engineer John Rennie, created huge economic opportunities. Horrocks, who had been a quarry-master, started a cotton mill in Preston which by the early twentieth century had grown into the largest in the world (there is a model of it in the Harris Museum and Art Gallery). Peter Todd also built a cotton mill and model workers' hamlet at Wheelton, the nearest village to us at Whittle Springs. The Cottons at Whittle had two branches, the cotton Cottons and the quarry Cottons. The cotton Cottons owned the mill at Whittle and by the early twentieth century also had mills for spinning and weaving cotton in Chorley and Black-burn. My great-grandfather's cousin Lawrence Cotton lived in a hard Accrington brick Victorian country house, 'The Pines' (now an ugly hotel with flat-roofed extensions), at Clayton Green and became Mayor of Blackburn. His eldest son was killed at the Battle of the Somme and his grandson in a car crash in the 1930s. In the same decade the textile empire of 6,000 looms and 70,000 spindles dwindled to nothing. Our Cottons developed the large gritsone quarry with its nine separate workings at Whittle Hills, manufacturing 'French' millstones which were dispatched down the canal to Liverpool and exported to the United States, Europe and the world. Though coarse, our stone was also used for

The quarries at Whittle: workmen with steam crane

construction, e.g. for the stone dressings at Crewe Station (I always pat them when waiting for a train), the foundations of the blast furnaces at Wigan, the mainline rail viaduct over the Ribble and the massive rusticated plinth of the Grecian Harris Art Gallery in Preston.

I have the quarry day books from the 1790s showing the tiny wages paid to the quarrymen, though there was some mechanization in the nineteenth century including a steam crane which I can just remember, abandoned in a water-filled crater. My great-grandfather, Ralph (pronounced 'Rafe'), sold up in the 1920s and died aged ninety-five in 1959. If only he had held on, we might have benefited from the post-Second War crushed stone boom for motorways. Planning permission was granted in 2003 to convert the abandoned workings into an artificial ski slope and leisurama – a metaphor for Lancashire.

When I was a child, the eighteenth- and nineteenth-century industry was already dead or going fast, but the waves of 1960s and 1980s suburbia, orange sodium light pollution and pointless motorways had not yet slashed or obliterated the picturesque landscape. The collapse of the industrial base and two world wars had left central Lancashire suspended in the 1950s like a stopped watch, with stone-built former industrial villages against the Claudian backdrop of the Pennines, often silhouetted by the low dazzling light of Northern winters, natural light but with the intensity of electric bulbs, while at night the hills were often still silhouetted by a halo of reflected orange light in the clouds from the industrial towns and cities round Bolton and Manchester thirty miles to the south.

I was born on 10 September 1948 in a now defunct private nursing home, St Joseph's in Mount Street, Preston. It was run by nuns. I think they were the Canonesses of the Holy Sepulchre, a recusant English community based (since the French Revolution) at New Hall, Essex, where they ran a girls' school. Clumsy and impatient from the start, I was two months premature, and came out feet first suffering from jaundice, a bright yellow baby with ginger fuzz on my head. My mother was horrified. My father thought me perfect. I was called John (after my great-uncle killed in the First World War) and Martin after St Martin of Tours, the patron saint of soldiers, who gave *half* his cloak to a beggar (i.e. a sensible, practical saint). My father had prayed to him during the war and attributed his delivery, partly, to St Martin's care.

I was one of the last generation of middle and upper class English boys to be circumcised as a matter of course: my mother was surprised by the unseemly witticisms of the nuns who reported that the doctor had found the operation rather difficult as 'it' was so tiny. (I was a small, premature, runt.) A recent convert, my mother was not at that time *au fait* with a specific Catholic brand of

JMR with mother, 1948

humour which finds anything to do with the body and 'natural functions' to be hilariously funny.

As it is now a historical footnote, it might be worth saying a few words about this obscure physiological offshoot of Empire. The fashion for infant male circumcision in England began in the 1880s and was energetically promoted by the British medical establishment for sixty years, on the grounds that it encouraged cleanliness and reduced the risk of cancer, though some thought it barbarous and unnecessary. Why did circumcision catch on? The most convincing theory is that the cut was an Indian Imperial fad. Circumcision had been practised as a treatment in the Army in India as far back as the eighteenth century. It was healthier and more comfortable not to have a sensitive foreskin in hot humid climates, and particularly so in itchy sandy countries, as the Jews and Muslims of the Middle East had long ago discovered. The end of the Indian Civil Service in 1947 and the economies of the National Health Service (which did not provide free circumcision) largely finished off the practice.

I value this personal souvenir of a vanished Empire. India was given its independence the year before I was born, but the other colonies and dependencies in Africa, Asia and the Caribbean still had years of active British rule. My first twenty or so years were lived under the shrinking baldachino of Empire. Many of my contemporaries at school came from abroad. Their parents were tea planters or farmers, colonial officials or medics or Army officers posted overseas. The boys' trunks were bright with labels from Kenya, Rhodesia, Ceylon, South America, Malaya and Hong Kong. During my (very brief) stamp-collecting phase I concentrated entirely on Empire and Commonwealth stamps, as my father and grandfather had done before me.

As a family we were Tories and Catholics. I still am – in a not entirely straightforward way. Not for me the Antonia White syndrome – 'the nuns were horrid so I lapsed and went mad'. Catholicism played a vivid role in my early life, and has continued to do so. My father's family was strongly Catholic. The Robinsons had married into old Catholic families on their return to Lancashire. The Elizabethan martyrs were close to us. Blessed Edward Bamber who had been hanged, drawn and quartered at Lancaster was a collateral relation. I knew the fields at Brindle (the adjoining parish to Whittle) where St John Arrowsmith had been captured and taken away to be tried and executed. It was all very near and very exciting. One could not have enough of the gory details of barbarous executions. We were proud of these brave Elizabethan friends, neighbours and relations who had died for the Faith. Father Faber's hymn 'Faith of Our Fathers' and R. H. Benson's *Come Rack! Come Rope!* thrilled us – the secret hiding places, the hasty Masses, the ancient missions in the hills once staffed by Jesuits and (still) Benedictines, all around. I pitied poor Protestants whose religion was colourless and boring and lacking such blood-soaked thrills. (We were not told much about Queen Mary Tudor's Smithfield bonfires.) At the age of five we longed for martyrdom; we all had our last speeches prepared ready for solemn delivery on the scaffold at Tyburn.

I made a church out of matchboxes, paper and flour paste. It was fully furnished with altars and candlesticks and enough paper vestments, painted in watercolour, in the five correct liturgical colours, for celebrating all the main seasons and feasts of the year. I was able to perform full-scale Masses, with a congregation of teddy bears, Martin (my cloth rabbit, without whom I couldn't sleep) and occasionally my reluctant sister Anne who did not share my liturgical enthusiasms then and certainly does not now. Eventually this cardboard church fell victim to hungry mice which ate it. Mice have a great taste for flour paste. Such things helped to develop my visual imagination. It is astonishing how many writers, painters and actors of a certain age in Britain were born Catholics, and regardless of their future religious inclinations or lack of them, first found an inspiration and stimulation in the ancient ceremonies of the Church. Gibbon got it right: 'The Catholic superstition, which is always the enemy of reason, is often the parent of taste.'

Our local parish church, St Chad, South Hill, dated from 1791.

The church was a cruciform structure with round arched windows, enlarged in 1812. A campanile and arcades of polished granite columns were added in 1898. It was the successor to a seventeenth-century Jesuit mission at Slate Delph, an old farmhouse on the other side of Wheelton. The priest was called Father Pilson. He was a good, shy, bustling little man, unswerving in his belief. I did not like him much. This was partly because when he visited our house he always tried to talk to me about soccer which I loathed and knew nothing about. Why did he not talk about churches and martyrs? Was that not his job? Poor man, he was just trying to make conversation and assumed that boys wanted to talk football (about which I suspect he knew little). He redeemed himself, however, in our eyes when one night the church caught fire. An electric fault in the organ ignited and destroyed the roof, leaving just a gutted shell. Very bravely, with a damp towel round his face to keep the smoke out of his lungs, Father Pilson crept into the blazing church and rescued the Blessed Sacrament from the tabernacle on the high altar. He was much admired by his parishioners for this daring act. We went to watch the smoking ruins the next morning and breathe in the pungent charred-pitch-pine-scented smoke. It was quiveringly exciting, and the story of the dramatic rescue of the consecrated Host from the flames made as much impression on us as the Miracle at Bolsena must have done around Orvieto in the thirteenth century. With such dramas seared into one's childish imagination, it has always seemed to me in retrospect a very second-rate thing to slough off religion just because the awesome symbolic literature called 'scripture' is not literally 'true', or some such suburban scruple.

The roof of the church was soon replaced, with quite a seemly plaster barrel vault, and the interior repainted in the bright ice cream colours beloved of Catholic churches. We stopped going there, however, because of an 'incident'. By that stage we had moved from Whittle Springs to the farm which was further away and were no longer within easy walking distance. One wintry morning my father drove us to church as usual. On a narrow, steep, icy brow at Copthurst we met another car coming in the opposite direction and had to slither backwards the full way down, and then very slowly zigzag all the way up again. We arrived late, a little flustered, and missed the Gospel. Father Pilson was already in the pulpit. He interrupted his sermon and glared at us as we were marched up the aisle to a seat at the front. 'Mass in this church begins at ten o'clock,' he pronounced. My mother loudly retorted 'I know it does. You are jolly lucky that we have come at all.' Stunned silence. In the early 1950s, in rural Lancashire, nobody answered a priest back. But then my mother was a 'convert' (she had abandoned her Protestant roots and joined the One True Church during the Second World War, thanks to Father Smythe, a Franciscan friar whom she had met while a driver in the WAAF). We children, pink with embarrassment, hid our heads below the back of the bench in front all through Mass in case the priest looked in our direction. Nearly fifty years later at my mother's funeral an old parishioner whom I did not know came up to me: 'We all admired your mother so much. She answered back.' The following Sunday, and from then on, we transferred our devotions to another church a couple of miles away, St Bede, at Clayton Green.

It is a sign of the rich Catholic history of West Lancashire that the countryside is dotted with Catholic churches every few miles. Clayton Green was then still a Benedictine parish, run from Downside. The priest was Dom Aidan Trafford OSB, a Downside monk who had also spent some years at Fort Augustus in Scotland. The church was a plain but elegant late-Georgian precursor of the Catholic Emancipation Act, having been built in 1823. The interior was a well-proportioned room with a flat ceiling and plaster cornice and central rose, and the Carrara marble altar was set in a rich alcove framed with Ionic columns. The whole atmosphere was different, not quite shabby, but definitely not bright. There were no gaudy colours as at South Hill. The walls were washed a pale blue, mellowed by years of incense and candle-smoke. There were silver candlesticks on the altar, not polished brass. The Lady statue was beautifully stencilled dark blue and gold in the Comper tradition.

Father Trafford was even more of a contrast. He did not wear natty, clean, black suits, nor did he bustle self-importantly around. He was tall and languid and spoke in an old-fashioned way – 'Marss' and 'Cártholic' – and was totally unselfconscious. He wore shabby old clothes when not in his Benedictine habit, hand-knitted grey pullovers unravelling at wrist and waist. When he got out of his car (a present from his sister), it was like watching a tape-measure unwinding from its case: he seemed to come out for ever, all bowed, before rising to his full height. He spent his days gardening, and intrigued us no end by pollinating the peaches in his little glasshouse with a fluffy rabbit tail. When he came to visit his parishioners, there was no stilted conversation about soccer. He talked with ease about haymaking, and books, the landscape and local history. Though I did not know then about such things as 'class distinction', I realized immediately that his dignified simplicity and the graceful threadbare quality of his house and church were 'patrician'. The liturgy, too, was different. We sang Gregorian Chant and there were a crucifer, thurifer and acolytes with candles. One had to remember to lower the processional cross when entering the sanctuary so as not to bang the hanging silver lamp in front of the altar. I loved serving Mass there, particularly for funerals as we were given handsome tips for doing so by bereaved families. We were also given tips for weddings, but I did not like them as much, all flowers and brides and silly girls in hideous frocks. The plainsong requiem, with its movingly simple *kyrie* and *sanctus* and the haunting 'Lux Aeterna' post-communion antiphon, is among my earliest musical memories, and a part of me.

Filius Sancti Benedicti Sum. I am sure it was partly through Father Trafford's influence that I went in due course to a Benedictine school, breaking the Jesuit tradition of my family; though my father was in any case determined that I should not go to Stonyhurst with its huge impersonal unstreamed classes, lack of school houses and sporty barbarism. I might have been happier if I had, because as it turned out the wrong Benedictine school was chosen for me.

I should hasten to add, before I am thought to be a crashing snob, that though I became one later, as a child I was not. A hyper-fine sense of social distinction, together with an assumed aestheticism, only developed in due course, as a defence mechanism against the more thuggish and hearty element at school. As a child I was totally free from any sense of social differences. I was a trusting, friendly little boy who did not hate or look down on anyone. My parents were almost simple-minded about such things, and let me mix freely, though emphasizing that we should not accept sweets or lifts from older strangers, ignoring the fact you are usually murdered by someone you know. In conversation they always said that social hierarchy was entirely historical in England, and that the last traces had been swept away by the Second World War. Even at the time, I thought this might be an over-optimistic (or pessimistic – depending on your point of view) assessment, but I kept such heretical thoughts to myself. I was allowed to run wild with the village boys. One of the most thrilling episodes was a game which went on all day, where we divided into two sides and hunted each other through the woods and hills, the canal tunnels and along the Lostock river bank for hours, until dark. It was so exciting. They all seemed very grown up to me, some of the older ones even smoking cigarettes. Afterwards my mother asked me whether they had sworn a lot. 'Oh no,' I said. 'No bloodys, or damns. They just kept shouting the name of those matches.' Puck was then a popular brand. She passed no comment.

From the age of four to seven I was an incorrigible television addict. I have never watched television since. Bill and Ben the Flower Pot Men, Andy Pandy and Little Weeeeed were personal friends. A production of *Tom Brown's Schooldays* with a jolly good thrashing in it perhaps first awoke a Rousseau-esque interest in spanking before I went to school myself. Like many English families we bought our first television set for the Coronation in 1953. The film of that event was the beginning of a lifelong love of British historic ceremonial, heraldry, the monarchy and all that went with it. The Coronation celebrations remain a very strong memory.

There was a village fête at Wheelton with patriotic red, white and blue bunting and a Punch and Judy show. All the children were given Coronation cups of an angular 1950s shape, reflecting the impact of the Festival of Britain. The detail I remember best was the ham sandwiches, into which sugar had escaped from the cakes – giving them an unpleasant, gritty, sweet taste and texture.

Not that we spent our days entirely glued to the box. We were primarily outdoor children. We had bantam chickens and a tame, crippled, wild rabbit. The fate of the latter fills me with dreadful remorse, and confirms the ancient view of the innate wickedness of children. I murdered it in a spasm of rage. I have always been subject to terrific fits of temper, difficult to control even with advancing years. The rabbit was called Hopalong and had only three legs. My father, who in another life should have been a gamekeeper, rescued him from a trap as a baby. He brought him home and nursed him; Hopalong became completely tame, our pet, and let us pick him up and hold him in our arms and stroke him. He was housetrained with a box of sand in the hearth of the dining room which served as his lavatory. We all loved him dearly. One evening my sister Anne and I quarrelled over who should hold him. Determined not to let her have him, I dashed him onto the hearth, broke his back and killed him instantly. My parents thought we had had an accident and dropped him, and commiserated with our tears.

I have less guilty memories of our bantam hens, though they too are permeated by sadness. The hens were fluffy and yellow with feathered pantaloons down to their feet and had a wooden hutch below the sitting room window, wandering free during the light in the uncut grass and weeds of the lawn. One day they had chicks. I opened the door to the hutch and, tweet tweet, there were all these extra miniature bantams, an astonishing surprise. My mother was thrilled by the excitement of my sister and myself. The chicks' father was my best friend Charlie. He was a magnificent specimen – like an eighteenth-century aquatint – greeny blue, orange and glossy black. He was a genuine Westmorland bantam fighting cock with long deadly spurs, and had been given to my father by the keeper at Whitbarrow Lodge near Catcrag. Though illegal, cock fighting was still prevalent in Westmorland in the 1950s and the farmers and keepers often bred these special birds. Perhaps they still do.

Despite his warlike genes, Charlie was tame, and friendly to me, and we loved each other unconditionally. This love was not shared by the neighbours as he would fly into their hen-runs and beat up their boring, cowardly ordinary cockerels. We had to clip his wings to stop these bellicose expeditions. He was eventually shot by poachers, who mistook him for a game bird. He just disappeared. I was distraught. My parents who knew the truth never told me what had happened. Life's later losses have lacked the same bitter sting.

The rabbits, fighting cocks, broody hens and general fauna and flora of home were by-products of my father's little shoot at Catcrag for which he bred the pheasants himself. I did not appreciate that other people did not have boiled pheasants' eggs for breakfast, or roast guinea fowl for Christmas. Catcrag was a small property on the Lancashire-Westmorland border in the Winster valley near Grange-over-Sands, a landscape reminiscent of Umbria in certain lights and seasons. It comprised a farm and bits of woodland. There was also the largest part of Nicholls Moss, an important natural habitat, renowned for its 300 species of moths or butterflies, and an SSSI of European importance, which now brings me terrifying responsibilities as its owner. I wake up thinking of butterflies, and hope they are breeding happily: the personal shame if they became extinct!

My grandfather had bought Catcrag from Canon Townley of Town Head whose family had owned it since the mid-nineteenth century. Before that it had belonged to the Wilkinsons. John Wilkinson, the famous ironmaster who is commemorated by a cast-iron obelisk at Lindale, one of the icons of the Industrial Revolution, had originally acquired this moss land on the north edge of Morecambe Bay, hoping to use the peat to fuel his iron blast furnaces. Peat did not give off enough heat so he drained and reclaimed some of the land for 'improved agriculture' instead.

There was a strong, stone-built early-nineteenth-century limekiln (now listed Grade II) used for burning lime to spread on the fields to counter the acidic soil. During the Second World War the peaty fields were used to grow celery and other vegetables, but this was not economic in peacetime, and the fields went back to grazing and hay. The first tenant was good, but when he left my grandfather's second tenant was lazy and incompetent. It was a joke that he would always greet us with an empty bucket dangling over his arm like a handbag but never seemed to do much work. The War Agricultural Commission tried to evict him for bad farming, but my grandfather resented this bureaucratic interference and defended him. This was an expensive mistake. It was to cost a lot of money getting rid of the tenant years later and making good his neglect.

This special place, which had something of the timeless, mysterious, numinous quality of a sacred Greek landscape, was very exciting for a child. There was a small network of caves in limestone, which had been inhabited in prehistoric times (my oldest house). It was easy to traverse them without getting lost. Nearby there was a medieval holy well, fed by a chalybeate spring and once a place of pilgrimage.

There were hundred-year-old anthills in the 'ancient enclosures' on top of the cliff. I literally got ants in my pants by sitting on one of these and digging into it, disturbing the inhabitants – a cause of much mirth to the onlookers. An old Scots pine tree had a rusty spade embedded in its upper branches. Some workmen must have parked it when the tree was small; and the tree had since grown, taking it upwards. The Scots pines were native and were descended from cones carried down in the peat from the tops of Cumbrian mountains by melting glaciers at the end of the Ice Age. There was a Second World War bomb crater in the peat, where a German plane had unloaded, mistaking us for Barrow.

I used to follow my father and his shooting friends round, and learnt how to hold and fire a gun, to clean and oil the barrel, to pluck and gut a pheasant. I probably gave my father hope that I would one day be as keen as he was. I also had an air rifle and practised shooting tins off walls. But I got bored and have never shot since I was eighteen. I was not good at it. However, early training once stood me in good stead in the CCF at school. A smart sergeant, who had marked me out (quite rightly) as a useless sissy, balanced a half-crown on the barrel of my rifle and bet me that I could not pull the trigger without shaking the coin off. He thought he was safe. I succeeded, and won his half crown. I savoured the astonishment on his face.

In general I was useless at anything practical. A farmer told my father: 'The trooble with that theer lad is he doan't shape.' I have never shaped. I don't drive, I hate all games, I don't type, I don't take photographs. I can hardly dial a telephone. I am the equivalent of dyslexic at anything practical. I was given a model pedal car when I was three or four, but couldn't work it, so let my sister Anne have it to drive round the house in. She was two years younger than I, but we were more like twins as I was small for my age. We were good friends as children and did much together, she taking the practical lead. She could be wildly irritating, almost to provoking murder. I once had the huge satisfaction of hitting her hard with a jagged tin bucket, cutting her head open. She ran streaming blood and tears to my mother, shrieking 'John did it.' As she always said this, nobody believed her, and I got away with it.

She could be extremely kind and generous when she wanted to, or when she was in the mood. In those days we did everything together, like two brothers – in some ways she was more of a boy than I was – including being ill together as we soldiered through the childhood course of measles, mumps and whooping cough. I rather enjoyed these sickness sessions as they merited fires (in the generally disused bedroom fireplaces), egg custards and grapes. Our bedrooms were usually freezing cold in the 1950s: the windows frosted over in winter and glasses of water turned to ice in the night just as in shudder-inducing Victorian memoirs. I am sure this helped to harden us, just as playing with farm animals and drinking milk warm from the cow inoculated us against germs. Ours was the last Spartan generation.

[29]

2

The Farm

My father had intended to move for some time, but it still came as a shock to us when it happened, especially as it meant an end to television – there was no electricity in the new house. We took over Hill Top in the winter of 1956. The farm tenant had given up the previous autumn, and my father embarked on his great adventure. Cattle, hens, sheep and pigs became part of our life. It was a disaster. Cows fell over the cliff into the quarry below. Hens and egg-production were destroyed by fowl pest epidemics and the Egg Board's idiocies. Farming, like most aspects of postwar economic life in Britain, was bedevilled by incompetent government interference and the whims of a multiplicity of 'marketing boards'. The egg market collapsed when the officials responsible decided that all English eggs should be stamped with blue lions, like English soccer shirts. The customer, rather than seeing this as a mark of quality, took it that the eggs were not fresh if they had been around long enough to be maculated in this way, and refused to buy them.

We kept a few free-range hens scratching around in a visible field, sunbathing in dust bowls and eating real worms. People would therefore stop to buy organic 'free range' eggs. The eggs for sale were actually produced in an Auschwitz-type battery complex, out of sight behind. My father had bought a derelict camp of Nissen huts from a dismal wartime site near Warrington. Heaps of old clapboard, loads of Crittal windows, a health 'n safety nightmare of asbestos sheets and other horrors were duly delivered to Hill Top and reassembled as a glorious eyesore: the 'Long Cabin'. It became one of my ambitions to demolish this encampment as soon as I was able and I did so much later. I hated the battery hens. They stank. They pecked each other's innards out through their bleeding bottoms. We were press-ganged into looking after them, staggering around with buckets of water sloshing into the tops of gumboots. Worst of all was cleaning the eggs, rubbing cement-like blocks of encrusted chicken shit from the shells with small wooden boards covered with sandpaper. If you pressed too hard, the shells broke and yellow yolk splashed all over your shirt, like a Beryl Dean needlework. The eggs had to be dry-cleaned as washing spoilt their freshness, or so it was claimed.

Cows were more attractive. The most maternal of animals, they mooed and lowed mournfully all night, keeping us awake, when their calves were taken away from them to be weaned. This process involved feeding with warm slush in buckets. You put your fingers into their food slop to remind them of udders and they licked them with pink or grey rasping tongues. They were charming. We were fascinated watching the male calves being castrated by the vet, or cows being 'i.v.ed' with test tubes, or the miracle of calves being born – the most effective form of sex lesson. I also learnt to milk a cow by hand. It is hard work.

Haymaking was best of all. Transient jobbing labourers, the sort of lost men who now beg in city streets, used to turn up to do the muck spreading, lambing and haymaking. They were single, silent, and self-contained, probably ex-Army; and travelled the country staying in hostels (in those days all towns had hostels for this type of transient labourer). They did paid piecework to buy cigarettes and drink. I can think of worse lives – at least in the summer. We rode around on the footplate of the tractor or sat on top of the hay cart. We were warned to keep away from the baling machine with salutary tales of people who had slipped and been dragged in, neatly chopped into two-foot lengths, and tied with bright twine. Once the baled hay was in the barn, it made a marvellous fort and was deliciously warm in the middle. I fell off the top of the hay cart and broke my arm. We all broke our arms on the farm. We spent much of our time being fixed in plaster or having anti-tetanus jabs. Hill Top was a dangerous place. I am covered with scars from barbed wire and sharp edges. Once I crawled behind some old wooden boards in the barn and a bent nail drove into my head. I was impaled and terrified. It had only penetrated between the skin and the skull so had not really gone in, but I couldn't move. My father gently unhooked me and it didn't bleed, much to my surprise. It has left me with a phobia about sharp metal points, and stabbing is the form of murder I least look forward to.

I used to wander round this heap of hideous shacks, muck and rusting machinery dressed in my great-grandfather's frock coat and top hat, like a Mad Hatter's tea party. The migratory labourers must have been bemused, but did not comment. Perhaps all the farms they went to were the same.

Hill Top Farm South, to give it the full postal address – for there was a Hill Top North, and the family also owned Hill Foot Farm – had been bought by my great-grandfather Aloysius after the First World War partly because of its connection with the Rainford ancestors who had lived there. It was an outlying part of the Cuerden estate sold off by the Towneley-Parkers in the 1920s. It straddled the parish boundary between Whittle-le-Woods and Brindle. Situated at 600 feet on the most westerly foothill of the Pennines (the White Hill in the Woods), it had a superb view south over the Lostock valley towards Wheelton and Heapey, Winter Hill and Anglezarke Moor (1,500 feet). The eighteenth-century folly tower on Rivington Pike and the Queen Victoria Jubilee Monument above Darwen formed symmetrical stops to right and left like vases on a cottage mantelpiece. A large radio mast took the place of the clock in the centre. It was a balanced classical landscape by Claude Lorrain or Gaspar Dughet and set standards of scale, symmetry and tone which few other views have matched. From the ridgeline at the top of our fields in front of the house there was an even more extensive but less picturesquely composed view westwards over the flat coastal plains and the Ribble estuary, with the Southport gasometer and Eiffel-like Blackpool tower prominent seaside landmarks about twenty miles away respectively. On a clear day the mountains of Snowdonia were visible to the south and the Lake District fells to the north, while the Isle of

Man shimmered in the distant sunset-stained salt waters. But I never saw Ireland beyond.

The house was early eighteenth century, long and low, of dressed local grit stone (from 'our quarry') with a stone flagged roof and a mixture of original mullion windows and later sashes. The barn was Georgian and the shippon Victorian. Only the stables of hard red Accrington brick were ugly, and I later demolished them with crowbar, sledgehammer and my own hands, as part of my adolescent anti-eyesore campaign, thus restoring the consistency of the local stone buildings. I broke a number of sledgehammers on these demolition jobs.

My grandfather had re-roofed the house and barn for the tenants in the 1940s, but nothing had been done inside. The house was wired and modernized by us, but that first winter we depended on paraffin lamps for lighting which gave an attractive greenish-glow and a not unattractive acrid oily smell. By the time the electricity came we had lost our taste for television and did not acquire a new one. The excitements and miseries of Cold Comfort Farm took its place.

The farm provided more than enough to keep children occupied. We used empty wooden ammunition boxes filched from the Royal Ordnance Factory at Euxton as homemade punts on the pond. In our teens we acquired an old Morris car and drove it round the fields. My sister Anne was expert and passed her driving test at first go. I, however, when I came to have driving lessons, found it difficult to navigate the narrow confines of real roads after the wide-open spaces, and have never learnt to drive. A surprising number of architectural historians do not drive. They are too busy looking at buildings to concentrate at the wheel. I tried to learn, but whenever I saw something interesting I tended to turn the car inadvertently towards it across the oncoming traffic, and thought it better for the safety of the human race if I did not persist. Anyway, I loathe cars and the ghastly, selfish, atomized society they represent. Walking, buses and trains are morally better.

There were now six of us at Hill Top. In addition to my parents and tomboy 'twin' Anne, I acquired two other younger sisters –

slobbering babies who were fed sticky, semi-liquid foods and porridges in their high chairs. They did not impinge on my life much apart from causing mild revulsion and encouraging Herod tendencies, which I have never shaken off. Once they grew into human beings, they became close companions and still are. Felicity ('Fiz') was aged one and a half when we moved. The younger, Jane Elizabeth, was born the first winter at Hill Top. She was named after St Elizabeth of Hungary to show my mother's support for the valiant Hungarians during their recent anti-Russian uprising in Budapest in 1956.

That was the year after the British general election, when my father had spent a good deal of time canvassing for the Tories. My grandfather ran the Preston North Conservative Association, and the MP since 1950 was Julian Amery, Macmillan's son-in-law. Every sinew was stretched to secure his re-election in that marginal seat. We conducted him around, drumming up votes. My grandfather, late in the day, remembered a Carmelite convent with fourteen nuns, and the prospective candidate went to see it. Julian Amery charmed the Mother Superior through a grille and she promised that her community would vote for him by post as they could not leave their enclosure. He was re-elected with a majority of fourteen votes after a recount. We shared all his political views, especially on foreign policy; preferring kings to presidents, Arabs to Israelis, and believing that coconut and palm were best off under benevolent British dominion.

My grandfather was historically minded. He had done some student schoolmastering in London before the First World War. I have his notebooks, in which he described the school in Fulham as being in an 'upper working class area'. During the First World War he had volunteered for the Navy (signals) and survived, but afterwards succumbed to parental pressure and the exigencies of married life, and entered the family business, J. & A. Robinson, though he considered wholesale cotton antipathetic. He was a good amateur artist in the apostolic succession of the English water-colour tradition, having trained under a pupil of David Cox. His

30. 3. 50.

Dear Mr. Robinson,

My wife and I want to thank you
personally for the magnificent work
you put in at the last election on
behalf of the Conservative cause.   A
candidate by himself can do very
little, and we both deeply appreciate
how much my victory has depended on
your unfailing support.

Thank you so much.

Yours sincerely,

Julian Amery

Julian Amery's letter of thanks

[35]

heart was really in Roman antiquities, Hadrian's Wall or the Catacombs, on which subjects he used to give talks to local groups.
After my great- grandfather's death aged eighty in 1939, he had
kept the business going through the war, just in case my father
survived and needed a job on his return. As it turned out, my father
preferred farming, so the old family business was closed down (my
mother was determined I should have nothing to do with it). The
warehouse was an eighteenth-century building of some historic
interest, and was therefore, of course, demolished by the town
council. The Jacobites were supposed to have held a council of war
there before the Battle of Preston, or perhaps it was Prince Charlie's HQ in 1745, anyway it had Jacobite associations. It was
compulsorily purchased in the 1950s (along with most of our other
property in Preston) to make way for a couple of hundred yards of
useless inner ring road. This disastrous planning error, which sliced
through the medieval street plan and wrecked the town centre, was
fought in vain by my grandfather as chairman of the Ratepayers'
Association. That, and the demolition of Gilbert Scott's magnificent
Victorian Gothic town hall, probably killed him. He died prema-
turely of cancer caused as much by the stress of this unnecessary
urban destruction, as by his smoking a pipe.

I remember the warehouse well: visits there were a childhood
treat. It smelt of brown paper and string, clean cloth, gas and Victorian soot. Chapel Yard was an eighteenth-century backwater, off
Friargate, one of the two principal old streets in Preston. At the end
was St George's Church, an Italianate C of E basilica. 'J & A's', as
we called it, had a five-bay, three-storeyed red brick domestic
frontage with an arch to one side, which led to the warehouse
behind with moon vests stacked in blue boxes or 'Hoghton Tower'
brands, my great-grandfather's registered trade mark, all ready for
distribution by van. The front door led into 'Reception', with
varnished 1920s woodwork, turned wooden barleysugar candlesticks on the chimneypiece, a gas fire, and Miss Nolan, my great-
grandfather's secretary, sitting in solitary splendour. (We paid her a
pension until she died.) Next door was the main office, run by Mrs

Craven, a friendly, jolly, maternal woman. My grandfather was 'Mr Joe', my father 'Mr Jack,' and I was 'Master John'. On the first floor was my great-grandfather's office with his kneehole desk, his chair and bookcase and gloomy oak framed lithographs of old Preston and a David Cox watercolour of Morecambe Bay Sands on the walls. It was a dusty, unoccupied room, until the aunts brightened it up in 'contemporary style': black and lime green paint with 'feature' wallpaper on one wall in 1950s magazine mode. I suspect this made my grandfather even more loath to use it. He tended to hold board meetings etc. at the accountants in Ribblesdale Place, a surviving Georgian building off Winckley Square which served as J & A's registered office. It still has a brass plate saying so, half a century after the firm was closed down. Upstairs again at Chapel Yard were neglected spaces, full of old family possessions, battered eighteenth-century books in tin trunks, a stuffed sparrow and chromolithograph of St Bernard dogs, which made delightful rummaging – stuff that had not sold at the ill-fated auction after my great-grandfather died in 1939.

I loved going to the warehouse for the day, and wandering to the barber in a little labyrinth of cobbled lanes behind St George's Church, all soon to make way for a desperate Arndale shopping centre with tango orange mosaic and a multi-storey car park dripping with concrete cancer. Had it been Chichester or Lewes, these alleys might have been preserved. But as it was the 'industrial North' nobody cared a toss, apart from my grandfather. Up to the late 1950s and 1960s, central Preston was a largely intact Georgian town with a medieval street plan and Victorian public buildings, like Lancaster (which by a miracle of inactivity has largely survived) but built of red brick rather than stone. There were huge nineteenth-century industrial quarters – mills and terraced houses – to east and west and posh twentieth- century suburbs to the north, but the old centre survived and could have been preserved; professional people and young families should have moved back to live in the Georgian houses round Winckley Square or in Fishergate Hill, in place of all the solicitors' offices and accountants. The postwar disaster of

England's provincial towns could have been avoided. It is no excuse saying that 'people did not know then'. Even at that age I knew it was wrong to flatten Georgian houses, smash Victorian Gothic stone carvings or slice through medieval streets. If others did not, it was 'culpable ignorance' in the Canon Law sense, and there is no justification, nor forgiveness, for them.

My grandfather lived just to the north-east of Preston at Heaton House, Ribbleton, a small cream-washed early-nineteenth-century house with a flat Tuscan door-case and symmetrical sash windows and castellated side bits concealing the old coach house and vinery. On the back of the house was a huge wisteria; rather intriguingly it seemed to grow out of a glazed brown drainpipe protecting its lower stem. This side of the house overlooked the lawn with my grandmother's rose beds to the right and the kitchen garden (behind a hedge) to the left. A herbaceous border with bright phlox divided the lawn from the orchard with rougher grass, apples, plums and pears beyond, and in the far corner was my grandfather's 'arboretum' – a stand of mixed trees planted to conceal the suburbs of Preston galloping remorselessly across the fields towards us. After my grandfather's death the inevitable happened and the town breached the defences and invaded the garden, though the house itself survived, truncated and spoilt. In other words my grandmother sold it for building development, as it was too close to the town. Fifty bungalows now cover the site. But I have recreated it in a safer place at Beckside near the northern Lancashire border, and with better architecture and the same pink and white phlox in the garden.

On visits to Heaton House we met my grandfather's friends, types from central casting – Major Dwyer and Monsignor Dunn. The Major had fought in the Burma campaign and was very pukka with a clipped moustache and a good stock of jungle stories. He gave me his swagger stick, a two-foot length of thick rattan which forms part of my collection of swords, whips and sticks in the front hall. The Monsignor looked like Cardinal Newman, ascetic and white-haired. Slight nicotine discolouring of the silver locks

At Heaton House, 1957: Anne, Felicity (behind) and JMR

hinted at blond youth. He was a Proto Notary, an exalted rank of
Monsignor and *ex-officio* member of the Papal Household (entitled
to wear a white mitre), like Alfred Gilbey who was to be a friend at
the Travellers' Club years later. Monsignor Dunn was also a
Cambridge man, but had been up before the First World War. With
hindsight, I can see that he was a classic Benson-type misogynist.
He told my sisters and me vivid biblical stories which my mother
thought were shockingly inappropriate for children. We particularly relished the end of Jezebel, thrown from the ramparts and
gnawed by wild dogs, 'so that her corpse was only identifiable by
her *painted* fingernails'. We thought this was delightful, and used
to repeat 'her painted fingernails' to ourselves with squeals of pleasure. Monsignor Dunn was the parish priest at St Gregory's,
Preston, where my grandfather was a governor of the school. (He
was governor of several Catholic schools in Preston.) We sometimes went to the Monsignorial church for the Corpus Christi
procession when my grandfather, in tails, starched shirt and white

tie carried the canopy over the Blessed Sacrament. The vision of the Monsignor in State on those occasions sticks in the mind, with his paper white complexion, and rustling lace and violet silk, like a painting by Velasquez or El Greco; or perhaps the Grand Inquisitor in *Don Carlos* at Covent Garden.

What was interesting about this aged *galère* was that they made no allowance whatever for children, but usually spoke over our heads. My grandparents did this too, and discussed our parents in ringing tones in front of us, assuming that we would not understand. This is a dangerous tactic, as children have excellent memories and though they may not fully take things in at the time, they remember and make sense of them later. Thus I came to understand my grandparents' disappointment in us, that we were 'badly' brought up, and that Whittle Springs and Hill Top were an incompetent mess, and that my father was 'hopeless with money'. This was true, but my father was a sweet and charming man with a childlike simplicity which endeared him to the young, and indeed everybody in general. My mother was admirably intelligent and complex, sentimental yet heartless, all attributes which I have inherited myself, though we were too identikit to get on. We kept our distances. I never kissed her after I went to school. I told her not to on the station in front of my friends, and that was that.

My grandmother had been strikingly beautiful as a girl. When I knew her, she was unwell, and had a morbid fear of bankruptcy. As a result she was given to pointless and extreme economies. Heaton House was stuffed with old boxes of matches and tins of syrup which she had hoarded during the war and then never used. She watered down the soup, the stew and the milk puddings when we went for lunch. She liked cards, and we played a game with her called Newmarket which I have never come across outside the family. We played for halfpennies. That a pious old lady felt so strongly about money that she wanted to win a simple game of halfpennies with her grandchildren was my first true insight into human nature.

I liked my grandfather. He looked rather like A. N. Wilson and wore battered trilbies, an editor's green eyeshade and old tweed coats, bound in leather. We shared interests in books, trees and buildings. He took me on driving trips to Wales or Scotland to look at ruins of abbeys and castles. He had the family charm and an eccentric directness. When we stopped for 'high tea' in a caff he would look at the menu and ask 'How many sausages do we get? Or rashers of bacon?' This made the waitress burst into giggles and give us extra – a good tactic. His car was a Javelin, a swept-down and forgotten Yorkshire postwar production, and a harmony of browns. The outside was pale brown. The inside was dark brown, with brown cloth upholstery and a strong smell of tobacco from his pipe which also seemed brown. This caused headaches and made me feel sick, which he attempted to assuage by giving me dark chocolate – the *coup de grâce*. I have never been able to eat chocolate as an adult.

All the family were car mad. My great-grandfather was among the first men in Lancashire to drive a motor, *circa* 1902, a Rover with a single-cylinder engine. He later had another (1918) Rover, two or three Daraques, an American Overland, and a Swift, his last car. When he died in 1939 he had fifteen cars jacked up in store. Sold as scrap they paid his funeral expenses. Even my grandmother drove, though she nearly gave up as a learner when she ran into a woman's dog. There was blood everywhere and piteous yelps. The owner was hysterical. It was difficult to decide which would expire first: dog, or mistress. My grandmother was nearly as distraught and vowed never to drive again. A vet was called to put the dog down. He wiped its face with a hanky. The dog got up, wagged its tail, and walked away. My grandmother had bust its nose; it was not otherwise harmed at all. Reassured, she then took to the wheel again with enthusiasm. My mother was also good with cars, and had been a WAAF driver during the war, while my father was absolutely mad about cars; he thought he was Stirling Moss changing down and roaring away, vroom, vroom. I was alone in the family in not driving and in my dislike of cars.

Buildings and architecture have been my passion from the dawn of memory. At the age of three or four I started sketching medieval churches and still have a drawing done at that age of the church tower at Canewdon in Essex. As well as architectural jaunts with my grandfather, the parents always encouraged my building mania, and all holidays were happily spent looking at old buildings after an unhappy experience at the seaside as a baby when I got sunburnt building a sandcastle on the beach and blistered so badly I spent the rest of the holiday in splints, bandages and iodine like an Egyptian mummified cat. Being very fair-skinned, I have never been able to stand the sun.

Redheads have one layer of skin less than normal people. This is the source of the joke about them having terrible tempers. They do get more easily irritated physically than the thick-skinned. Red hair is one of the genetic physical characteristics thought to have evolved through climate, and is the opposite of black skin which developed in hot areas to keep the sun out. Red-haired people emerged from the far North, in the Arctic Circle, and their thin skin developed up there to let in as much rare sunlight and its life-giving vitamins as possible. In the British Isles 'ginger' is most prevalent in the Celtic and Viking Northern fringes – Trans-Trentine England, Ireland or Scotland – where many of my ancestors came from. Like intelligence (or great height), red hair is a recessive gene and you need it on both sides for it to continue. My mother was dark and my father blond – on the farm we teased him that the cows licked and nibbled his head because they mistook his hair for hay – but both my grandfathers had once been red-headed, though grey when I knew them. My father always claimed that his hair was bleached by the sun in North Africa and Italy during the war, after he ran away, straight from school, at the age of eighteen and joined the Desert Air Force, where he expressed his architectural talents in building camouflage sites for the enemy to bomb, and his love of motorized speed by zooming round the sand dunes on a powerful bike. Lawrence of Arabia was a lifelong hero. He was then one of a group from the Desert Air Force attached as support to Montgomery's Eighth Army, and continued all up Italy from the Sangro

JMR's father in uniform, aged eighteen

River to Klagenfurt in Austria, where he finished the war. I suspect those were the happiest years of his life.

My hair was the darkest red of the four children, and that of each of my three sisters was lighter according to their descending ages: the youngest being blonde. I told them with tongue-in-cheek sibling superiority that the colour ran out as it went down, like the brains. I have always had a love-hatred for ginger hair. In my 'salad days' (a Shakespeare and not Noël Coward phrase) I would have preferred to have been tall and dark and handsome, preferably a seven-foot, beautifully muscled, strong-featured negro like Caspar the third king in *Quattrocento* Epiphany paintings. In middle age I thank God for the subtler, more long-lasting physical characteristics I was given – health, clear skin, goodish teeth and excellent eyesight so that in my fifties I do not yet wear glasses. And one was not entirely hideous in a cheerful, cherubic puck sort of way. Secretly, I am quite proud of my distinctive appearance and features and am glad to be a *rara avis*. In fact, it would be difficult to be more of a minority figure than a ginger, circumcised, intelligent, lower-upper-class Brit. I relish the rarity.

Childhood holidays were always spent in East Anglia where my mother's family had come from, and some distant relations still hung out. We spent our days looking at pargeted cottages, flinty priory ruins, medieval churches and the Norman keep at Castle Hedingham. Or sometimes, for a change, collecting cockles and mussels which were fun to dig out of the sand, but disgusting to eat. The rolling, arable, oak-treed landscape, and the muddy, many creeked estuaries of the Blackwater and Orwell, and the sea-wide mouth of the Thames with silhouetted wartime defences were all a cheerful contrast to Lancashire. We never went abroad in my childhood; my father had 'done that' during the war. It was always hot and sunny in Southern England and my strongest memories are of the sickly scent of privet hedges in flower, and the tang of warmed greasy metal: unromantic, dingy English smells that have the power of Proust's Madeleine to transfer me back to *temps perdu*. We also went to London a lot where the streets were still heroically pockmarked with bombsites; the overture being the sulphurous whiff of steam trains in vast smoky Victorian stations. How one regrets old Euston. I cannot honestly say that I can remember Thomas Hardwick's monumental Grecian propylaeum in front (vandalistically demolished by Harold Macmillan), though I must have passed it dozens of times.

My childish architectural sympathies were medieval or Tudor. Classicism came with puberty. My strongest baby memory of London is of tall sharp-cornered wedge-shaped buildings glimpsed through taxi windows, probably the area north of Victoria Station, the Mappin & Webb building in the City (demolished by Peter Palumbo), or Grand Buildings in Trafalgar Square, and, of course, the battlements and ravens of the Tower of London. Both Westminster Abbey and Westminster Cathedral (one formerly 'ours' and the other now 'ours') were favourites. I have vibrant memories of the cloisters at Westminster Abbey, glimpses of green through tracery, and the dark subaqueous gloom of the vaulted passages leading to the Little Cloister, lit by gas, and overhung with green creeper at the far end. The undercroft with dusty waxwork images of deceased sovereigns and consorts made more of an impact than the magnificent Baroque marble tombs which I must have edited out in those blinkered pre-Georgian days. Most important was the general air of antiquity. The place was always in scaffolding. I was deeply impressed when my father told me that a building as old as the Abbey needed continuous repair. I thought that meant the scaffolding was permanent; that the place would collapse instantly if masons and carpenters put down their hammers, saws and trowels for a minute, and that their feverish activity would be necessary round the clock for ever and ever. In fact, what we saw was probably the early stages of the postwar beautification of the Abbey under the direction of successive surveyors, notably Stephen Dykes-Bower – gilding the lily rather than essential structural repair.

Westminster Cathedral was a source of awesome wonder, though only fifty-five years old. Just as Westminster Abbey required 'constant work to stop it falling down', the Cathedral 'would take

hundreds of years to complete'. Though golden mosaics and gleaming marble revetments were still being applied to the lower levels of
the interior in the 1950s, the blackened brick, Piranesian gloom
above the snow line looked an infinite task ever to be finished (I
hope it never is). Whereas the Abbey, seen through the prejudiced
eyes of boyhood, was now secular and all about the glory of the
monarchy, the Cathedral with its flickering candles, devout, kneeling worshippers and atmospheric side chapels was where God had
moved to, conveniently along Victoria Street. It had an aspect of
home from home. The Cardinal, Archbishop Godfrey, confirmed
me. In a glass box lay the quartered remains of St John Southworth
from Samlesbury near Preston, one of the martyred Lancashire
neighbours. My grandfather gave me the Pitkin guidebook, a splendidly written job by Canon Bartlett (uncle of Jennifer, the Fat Lady
cook) and Bishop Gordon Wheeler. I remember a particularly
arresting sentence about the carving of the marble side altar in the
Vaughan Chantry which showed 'how robustly *verde antico* can
take the chisel'. What luck that an unimaginative editor's blue
pencil had not crossed through this archaic form and left poorer
gruel for the architectural neophyte to swallow. My imagination
was caught and nearly all I know about different marbles comes
from the Cathedral. It had been the aim of the architect, J. F. Bent-
ley, to display an example of as many different marbles as possible
and there were already nearly one hundred in place, with their
wonderful names – Porphyry, Cipollino, Verde Antico, Alabaster,
White Pentelic, Breccia Violetta, Rosso Rubino, Pavonazzo, Breccia, Veronese, Languedoc, Bardolino, Carrara – redolent of the
glory that was Greece and Rome.

We did not always go south by train. My father preferred to
drive. In pre-motorway England the journey took all day. The
Preston bypass, Britain's first motorway, was opened by Harold
Macmillan, and the south part of the M1 in 1959, but the rest of
the North-South network was not completed for at least another
ten years. At first it speeded things along, before the traffic silted up
again, as it always does. In the 1950s we drove down the A6 and

A5 (one an early nineteenth-century turnpike, the other Roman). It was not a picturesque journey as it traversed some of the ugliest parts of Europe, the derelict South Lancashire coalfields, the Potteries and the fringes of the Black Country, all now mercifully bypassed by well-designed new roads. The informal landscaping of the first-generation motorway network with native trees, rough cut grass and wild flowers is one of the visual improvements in which the English should take pride. Those well-designed banks could easily have been a welter of mown phosphorescent lawn, dwarf golden shrubs, pink begonias and deathly *Cupressus leylandii* like the terrible gardens one now sees in so many villages. Whoever was responsible for this excellent, understated work in the best eighteenth-century landscape tradition deserves canonization.

We always had a halfway break at Lichfield where we stopped for lunch and, of course, to look at the cathedral. As a result Lichfield is one of the medieval fanes I know best, though much of the glory comes from Gilbert Scott's Victorian restoration. The magnificent fittings, tiles and ironwork by a fluke have survived, unlike their counterparts at Salisbury and Hereford which were scrapped to make way for beige carpets and splashed poached-egg altar frontals. Lichfield is an ideal cathedral for a child, not too big and the architecture harmonious; nor did the merely plaster vaults and mass-produced west front statuary disappoint the untutored eye. I was once gazing at the cocoa-coloured façade when the bishop popped out and finding a junior architectural enthusiast on his doorstep (and in those days Anglican clergy were educated) kindly stopped and pointed out that one of the seemingly symmetrical spires is three feet shorter than its twin. I had never noticed before.

Despite the slowness of the journey and the hideousness of much of the Midlands landscape, we children did not grow fractious or bored – partly because of the sense of adventure and travel, but mainly because my mother had devised a very good game to keep the back seat occupied. This was compiling lists of fifty objects: church spires, castles, pubs, bulls, swans… The winner was the one with the most sets of fifty things. Lichfield with its three spires on one building was an obvious fillip to the spire count, and we nearly always filled our swan count at the bridge at Bedford. Perhaps I ought to patent this quiz as a children's car game? I would recommend it, anyway. It fills hours. Another occupation, before car book tapes, was to read aloud. We did all the Hobbits in this way: *The Lord of the Rings* lending itself to dramatic rendition on the move. My mother was a good clear reader and both parents entertained us with books as young children. Since I first learnt to read over fifty years ago, I have always had my nose in a book – the current book on the boil being like a cook's stockpot. Reading adds another dimension to life, and is a foolproof antidote to the minor irritations and longueurs of daily existence. It is tasteless (and pointless) to criticize parents. They were what they were. One is what one is. Whatever else, I am eternally grateful to mine for encouraging a love of books and reading.

My grandmother was told categorically by a young doctor that because of her pelvic structure she could not have children. 'But I have three,' she protested. In a way, however, the doctor was right. She had six babies altogether, but three only lived a few hours, because their heads had been crushed during birth. My father lived but was always simple. Though good at sport and art, at school he was the despair of his Jesuit masters. The institutionalized certainties of the war, and then 'farming' afterwards, carried him through to middle age, where my mother took control of the budget, and paid the bills, and gave up hope. By then I had escaped.

The main argument in favour of boarding school, however ghastly, is that it gets you away from your family and the constraints of home. It allows you to develop independent views and judgements, and widen your mind and circle of friends, beside which inestimable gifts a little transient torture seems a small price to pay. There is also the possibility, I suppose, of some 'education', but that tends to come more from peer grouping and autodidactism than the formal curriculum. It is a miracle that anybody picks up a smattering of learning. I began my formal 'education' at the local primary school, St Chad's, South Hill, where I spent a year before my parents took me away and sent me somewhere better. All I remember of my scholastical initiation is sitting at a little desk in a large Victorian room, having learnt with much sweat, blood and tears, to write 'John', and despairing of ever being able to manage 'Robinson'. It is my 'real school', later, that sticks in my memory with all the force of a Hollywood horror movie. It was called Fort Augustus Abbey and was situated in Inverness-shire in North Britain.

3

Gothic

My school was the most northerly Benedictine establishment in the world. I was educated on the same latitude as Tobolsk. Thanks to the Gulf Stream, and the central location in the Great Glen, the climate was surprisingly mild, except in the depth of winter. There was half the rainfall of Fort William, thirty miles to the west, and none of the icy winds of the east coast. May and October were memorably beautiful months. It was possible to forget the northern latitude, but there were occasional reminders, especially the fact that apples would not ripen because of the curve of the earth and the consequent lack of sunlight in late summer, and the distant mountains were sometimes snow-capped. This did not bother us in the least. The main drawback on the water-girt site was the onslaught of midges on summer's evenings.

Nor was the place especially uncomfortable by the standards of austere, all-male establishments in the 1950s and 1960s. The buildings were warm and there was plenty of hot water, with oil-fired boilers maintained by Brother Wilfred, a plumber of genius, somewhere in a distant vault. It was in many ways more comfortable than home, which did not have central heating. The Abbey had a tradition of advanced technology and had been the first institution in Scotland to have electric light, with its own hydro scheme installed in 1889. The place was, in many ways, still self-sufficient. It ran the local fire brigade with a glossy scarlet fire engine in a garage off the kitchen court and one of the monks serving as fire master for the area. The Abbey baked its own bread, had its own printing press and still in those years had a large staff of lay-brothers, as well as sad, pious, humourless Poles washed up in Scotland in the aftermath of the Second World War. The lay-brothers included cooks, a barber and proper apprentice-trained plumbers, carpenters and other craftsmen and technicians. Before the war there had even been shoemakers and a German confectioner.

Topography can be the nursery of artistic imagination. I think of those English poets and their love of landscape: Wordsworth and the Lake District, Housman and Shropshire, John Clare and Northamptonshire. Regrettably, the Highlands have always left me cold. Formative years spent there have given me the strongest possible admiration for the landscape of Hertfordshire and Surrey. Yet the site was sublimely splendid. I have lived in many beautiful places, but none was as spectacularly, classically, beautiful as Fort Augustus. The Abbey was situated at the west end of Loch Ness. There were uninterrupted views along the deep, cold, monster-inhabited waters for almost thirty miles towards Inverness, framed by mountains and forests. Behind stretched the Great Glen of Albyn and the peaks of Ben Tee and the Glengarry Hills. Few large buildings, not just in Britain but in Europe, have such a picturesque setting. The Abbey itself was also impressive in a Victorian Pugi-nesque manner, with traceried Gothic cloisters, carillons of bells, three towers, one rising to 140 feet, and a cathedral-scale church.

'Why did your family send you to such a remote place?' I am often asked. Well, they had a Queen Victoria reverence for the Highlands of Scotland. Though 400 miles from home, it was really quite convenient for North West boys going to school by train, just a straight line to the Polar region. Downside would have meant travelling to London and changing to the Great Western. Heaven knows how one would have got to Belmont in Herefordshire. Worth had not yet got off the ground. It was, of course, almost impossible to go across country by rail to York for Ampleforth, so once Stonyhurst had been discounted, Fort Augustus was the 'nearest school' in the 'nobody between us and the Locker-Lampsons' sense. The Royal Scot express train raced to Glasgow, and then the West Highland Line meandered through the Grampian Mountains round the moors and lochs to Spean Bridge near Fort William. (Luggage was sent in advance, as was the norm.)

The real reason was that the charismatic, ambitious Abbot of

Fort Augustus in the 1950s, Dom Oswald Eaves, was a Lancashire man and friend of my grandfather's. His name was the same as that of his kinsman, a well-known recusant English Benedictine in the seventeenth century, which is why it may seem faintly familiar. During his reign, considerable expansion had taken place, the long-delayed nave of the church built to the design of Reginald Fairlie (work had stopped during the First World War), new wings added to the school, tourist shops established (with a strong Loch Ness Monster element and ringing cash tills). He was keen to build up the school and wrote round to all his friends and connections asking them to send their sons, grandchildren, nephews, godchildren and anybody else they knew. My family complied. Unfortunately his go-getting style did not go down well with the conservative monastic community, and the year I arrived at school he was voted out and replaced by a cabal of reactionaries under the Abbacy of Dom Celestine Howarth – the beginning of a disastrous chain of events which within forty years was to destroy the whole place, school and abbey. Abbot Oswald Eaves went off to be a Catholic missionary in Sweden, and I arrived as a new boy at this strange grey Gothic pile in its surreally beautiful setting in the far North.

The Abbey of St Benedict at Fort Augustus was the only foundation of its kind in Scotland, though it was part of the English Benedictine Congregation. Its antecedents were noble *in excelsis*. It was the successor to the ancient abbey of St James of the Scots at Ratisbon, in Bavaria, a renowned seat of learning in the Middle Ages, and in the recusant period, and of the English abbey of SS Adrian and Denis at Lamspringe near Hildesheim, the senior English recusant Benedictine house. It occupied the site of a fort built originally in 1729 and reconstructed after the '45 rebellion when it had been blown up by Bonnie Prince Charlie's troops. Fort Augustus was named after the Duke of Cumberland, youngest son of George II and 'butcher' of Culloden, who described Fort Augustus as 'this diamond in the midst of hell'. I was not so sure about the 'diamond'. It was the centre of the road system laid out in the

1720s by General Wade to pacify the clans and map the mountains (the beginning of the Ordnance Survey), and commanded all the roads and passes of the central Highlands. To the south stretched the Corrieyairack Pass at 2,500 feet, through the bleak wilderness towards Perthshire. To east and west the chain of lochs, once patrolled by English ships of war, connected with other forts: Fort George at Inverness (named after the Hanoverian Pretender) and Fort William (after wicked Billy, victor of the Boyne) to the west. These were later linked by Thomas Telford's Caledonian Canal with its staircase of six locks at Fort Augustus. Everything about the place was Georgian and Victorian imperial; at least the past was. The present was dreary, laddish, and second-rate; terrifying and boring in equal measures. Perhaps it was these school years which impressed on me so strongly the tragedy of Britain, from idiosyncratic glory to degraded American suburb.

Fort Augustus under Jerome Vaughan and Oswald Hunter Blair had been the smartest Catholic school in Britain in the 1880s and '90s, just as Newman's Oratory School had been in the 1860s, or Ampleforth under Dom Paul Neville was to become in the 1930s. Schools are like restaurants: they depend on the chef. But that high point had been sixty years earlier. The reality in the early 1960s was quite other: most of the boys were Scottish thugs or colonial expatriates, and some of the masters seemed to me certifiably mad. Academic standards were not high, and compulsory rugby and champion-standard hockey were the be-alls of existence. The day-to-day atmosphere of the school was philistine, though the Abbey was not. It took me decades to recover from the academic disabilities, and I have never recovered from some of the other things. I became a crippling snob in self-defence, and this caused a regrettable narrowing of sympathies which only London eventually erased. I learnt one new thing there – hate. I had never hated before. I did not know before what it felt like to want to kill somebody, to annihilate, to destroy a person. It is, of course, very character-forming that one should develop such passions. I am often struck by the blandness of other people, with their vacant, trusting countenances. They were not tormented by 'Dolly' Mackenzie and his fellow prefects.

Dolly had been kicked in the head during a game of rugby and seriously concussed; he had been in a coma for months. I wished he had died. When he eventually came round, in compensation they let him stay on for another year, as a special treat, and made him a house prefect (an early form of care in the community). He was put in charge of the junior boys in Lovat House, my house.

His head was round, like a ball (no doubt why it was kicked), the perfectly-formed features and sleek black hair curiously artificial, the complexion waxy, the stare glassy-eyed. Hence his nickname, the use of which (by his underlings) contained not a splinter of affection. He wore a watch chain and funny waistcoats, a prefectorial privilege. He exuded an aura. When you met him in a corridor or on the stairs it was like finding yourself trapped by a poisonous reptile. There was the same slow, hypnotic pause before the deadly pounce. 'Go to your house master. Twice three.' 'But, Mackenzie. Why? I wasn't doing anything.' 'Don't argue, boy. Twice six.' One of his duties was looking after our dormitory. This added an intensity to our bedside prayers, as we knelt in stripy pyjamas on the shiny pine boards. 'Please God, don't let Mackenzie be in a bad mood tonight.' He once had the whole dormitory beaten on a whim. He had no power to beat himself, he could only refer, but nobody queried his decisions. 'You disgusting little boys. You haven't washed.' 'Yes we have, Mackenzie,' we wailed piteously. 'You're lying. Go, downstairs and wash.' So off we all trooped, for the second time, to the basement ablutions, hung around for a minute and went back upstairs to the second-floor dormitory. He was glaring, watch in hand. 'You're all late,' he said slowly. 'Go to your house master.' There was something mesmeric about him, so we did; and got six each.

On another occasion, when he was sitting at the head of our table in the boys' refectory, like a capricious caliph, he hurled a pot of salt down the board. It landed in front of me; he told me to stay behind and count the grains after lunch (i.e. waste my most valued free time, when we were encouraged to go for walks before after-noon lessons began again after tea). Two hours later I reported to Mackenzie: '2,533.' 'You're lying, boy. Count it again tomorrow afternoon.'

The task he enjoyed most was taking us for runs. It reminded him, I suppose, of his glory days on the rugger field as captain of the First XV. In his shorts and red shirt with the head of St Benedict's pet raven or corbie[1] embroidered on his breast (the school colours), we would find him jumping athletically around outside the Tower Entrance, stop-watch to hand, as we emerged reluctantly into the cold wet, shivering in skimpy rugger kit, and retching inwardly. We went on runs in the afternoons when the weather was too bad even for games, that is, in sleet and snow, titanium hard frosts, and torrential downpours. I loathed runs at the best of times. But a Mackenzie run had many refinements of misery. He would drive us up the steepest mountain sides and then make us do press-ups at the top while we were still gasping, crippled with stitches and ready to collapse. He darted around at the back shrieking 'On, boys, on!' like a farm dog nipping the heels of a lazy cow. I would never want to go on a run again, and am always amazed to meet otherwise sane young professionals jogging spontaneously and contentedly in London streets.

The regime had a more drastic effect on one sensitive English boy. He was made so miserable that he determined to burn the place down. He went without leave to the village (a sign of absolute desperation, as it was a beatable offence in itself) and bought a gallon of meths from Leslie's Stores. In the early hours he crept downstairs in his slippers to the basement; to the stygian place where all our trunks were stored, and poured the meths over them. He then threw in a match and whoosh – the whole place went up in flames. We were woken by the fire alarm at 2 am and pat, according to the fire drill, marshalled ourselves in School House order, in our dressing gowns, in the cloister garth where we had the delightful

[1] According to legend, St Benedict's tame raven had saved him from poisoning by snatching away the deadly bread in its beak.

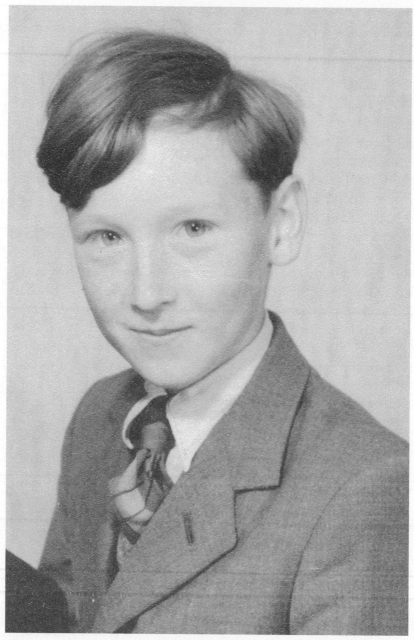

JMR aged fourteen

prospect of black smoke pouring from every window and orifice, and fleeing monks out of the Abbey wing, pulling on their habits as they emerged. Sadly, the basement was mainly vaulted – a relic of the old fort – and the fire was soon brought under control by the Abbey engine with little serious damage done to the school's fabric. Term continued on its remorseless grind, and the arsonist disappeared that very morning, never to be heard of again. He probably went to Eton or somewhere. There was the usual cover-up. Our parents were told about a 'small cellar fire' (and, by the way, could they buy new trunks on their household insurance?) but there was no official report of how it was started or why.

The prefects at Fort Augustus were called the Pots and their den of authority the Pots' Room. It was halfway up the front stairs on the first floor of the baronial-style School Tower with an oriel window commanding views of the grounds to north, east and west. It smelt of leather (rugger balls), sweat and burnt toast. ('You silly little idiot, you've done it again. 3,000 lines.') It needed to be given a very wide berth. The Pots were nearly all ghastly, even if Mackenzie was the worst. One way of avoiding them was to plan elaborate routes circumnavigating the building, excluding the front stairs and the dread proximity, thus instilling a sense of architectural topography and a facility with plans and maps.

Boys are naturally conservative and there was a lot of Victorian and 1920s schoolboy sartorial detail and vocabulary still in general currency, like the neo-medieval 'Jakes' for latrines or 'bogs'. I was told as a leg-pull that this was Greek and short for *bogoi*. When you left your shoes for repair by the village cobbler, you placed a strange note in them: 'Thank you and oblige'; and Matron was always called 'Kitty' regardless of her real name.

Matron for most of my time was Mrs Coppin; a naval wife type and the soul of brisk, sensible kindness in a fetching starched uniform. She once let me stay in bed in the Infirmary, on the edge of the grounds, for a week, after I sprained my ankle badly, jumping downstairs to the basement, avoiding a Dolly-like monster. This brief respite in a haven of unschool-like comfort, eating better food, being visited only by solicitous friends, and generally avoiding the horrors, provided a good opportunity to read about country houses in back copies of *Country Life*.

There were the usual hierarchies and cultivated oddnesses – especially in the clothes department. The cricket blazer was a retina-sizzling collector's piece – bright red with black and white chequered edging and St Benedict's corbie on the pocket. It was an astonishing sartorial survival, *en suite*, with the pretty red and white painted cricket pavilion. It had been invented by Abbot Macdonald in 1922, inspired by the scarlet and white colours of Corpus Christi College, Cambridge, and symbolic of the Eucharist. We only wore these vivid blazers (and matching caps) for cricket, expensive extravagance for our parents. Belts were disapproved of, and we were not allowed to wear them. If your white cricket flannels were loose at the waist you were expected to keep them up with a school tie knotted in front. In an irrational way, I have maintained this absurd shibboleth all my life, and consider belts in trousers to be unspeakably naff. I remain a braces man myself. I suspect this was a survival of a genuine Victorian snobbery, from when only real working men wore leather belts. It is astonishing that it flourished with such sap-like freshness in the 1960s.

On Sunday the English wore dark or grey suits and the Scots the kilt in their own dashing clan tartan which gave them a distinct advantage over us and caused pangs of envy as we were upstaged by Hunting Stewart and all the rest. Junior boys wore grey flannel shirts; senior boys white shirts. The school tie was a design of thin diagonal stripes, red, black and white, subtly differentiated between houses. On weekdays we wore grey trousers and Lovat tweed coats, a sort of feudal livery. Lord Lovat was the Abbey's founder and lay-patron. Lady Lovat (and presumably her daughters) as 'founder's kin' were the only women allowed into the monastic enclosure in the east range of the cloisters, so we were told. I do not remember them ever coming to exercise their unique privilege, but the imminence of this august feminine invasion contributed a nice Alice-in-Wonderland detail. Our contact with the female sex was largely restricted to the school holidays, though we did occasional joint theatricals and concerts with the girls of Inverness Academy, and had a semi-detached relationship with the Convent of the Sacred Heart at Kilgraston, Perthshire, where many of the boys' sisters went to school and where there was an annual dance for the Fort boys and the Kilgraston girls.

The establishing of a Benedictine monastery in 1876 on the site of the redundant Hanoverian fort at the head of Loch Ness was the vision of Dom Jerome Vaughan (brother of the Cardinal), the 15th Lord Lovat and the 3rd Marquess of Bute. Lord Lovat gave the site, Lord Bute contributed the money, and Jerome Vaughan was the first prior of the new community. There were other noble benefactors including the Duke of Norfolk and Marquess of Ripon. The *éminence grise* behind the development of the project in the late nineteenth and early twentieth centuries, however, was Dom Oswald Hunter Blair, OSB, *alias* Sir David Hunter Blair, 5th Baronet of Dunskey (1853–1939). Hunter Bunter – as we irreverently thought of him – was a characteristic Victorian romantic and Oxford convert to Catholicism. The inspiration for his conversion to Rome came not from some piercing theological insight, but, more sensibly, was the result of youthful reading of the novels of Sir Walter Scott (his grandfather had been Scott's banker), with their sympathetic picture of medieval religion and the brave Catholic knights of old. Montalembert's *Monks of the West* inspired him to become a Benedictine. Hunter Blair was up at Magdalen, Oxford, in the same generation as Oscar Wilde whom he knew well. He was a friend and neighbour of Lord Bute's (when Bute was at Dumfries House) and shared his vision for the revival of monasticism in Scotland. He entered the Benedictine Order at the new Fort Augustus Community when it opened in 1878. He sold the Hunter estate and charming Georgian house of Dunskey in Wigtownshire which he had inherited. Blairquhan, the Blair seat in Ayrshire, was entailed and he transferred that to his younger brother, an officer in the Navy; it still belongs to the family. He gave all the proceeds from his patrimony to the Benedictines. He personally paid for the Pugin cloisters, and brought the furniture from Dunskey to Fort Augustus where Regency mahogany wine coolers, wig-stands and elegant tables settled incongruously into the Gothic setting but underlined the country house element in the hospice (guest house) and Abbey proper. The school, by contrast, was always very much behind the green baize door, with its independent, rougher facilities.

The laconic description of Abbot Hunter Blair in *Burke's Peerage and Baronetage* captures something of his aura: 'educated Eton and Magdalen College, Oxford (M.A. 1878), entered Benedictine Order 1878, ordained 1886, Rector of Abbey School, Fort Augustus 1890–95, Master of Hunter Blair's Hall, Oxford 1889–1909, Abbot of Fort Augustus 1913–17, titular Abbot of Dunfermline, was Priv. Chamberlain to Pope Leo XIII, late Capt. Ayr and Wigtown Militia.' I find the last detail especially delicious. In his brief military career he also served as a Papal Zouave in Rome. As well as Fort Augustus, Hunter Blair was involved in two other Victorian monastic establishments. He was the first Master of the English Benedictine house opened in Oxford in 1889 (now St Benet's Hall) as he was the only British monk at the time with an Oxford MA, being a convert. (Cradle Catholics did not attend English universities for much of the nineteenth century because of religious restrictions, on both sides.) In 1909 he was succeeded as Master at St Benet's by Dom Anselm Parker who was in Oxford until 1920 when he became Head Master of Fort Augustus.

He also helped to revive the Benedictines in Brazil with a new abbey and convent in the city of São Paulo, which still flourishes, with his portrait hanging in the refectory, and the restored abbey of S. Bento amidst a grove of coconut palms at Olinda. This Firbankian dream was centred on a Portuguese Baroque church with a huge gilt reredos. There little Indian boys from the jungle were taught to sing Gregorian Chant (do they still?). The Arts and Crafts Workshops in São Paulo produced the beautiful rosewood screen for the Blessed Sacrament Chapel at Fort Augustus, through Hunter Blair's direct patronage.

When the Scottish climate was beginning to affect his health 'the Abbot' (as his family always referred to him) tended to spend the winters in Brazil (despite the vampire bats) and summers at Fort Augustus (despite the midges). He was a prolific man of letters. His three volumes of memoirs – *A Medley of Memories, A Further Medley of Memories,* and *A Last Medley of Memories* were a source of almost hysterical delight to me. There were disregarded stacks of them everywhere, and they provided an escape into a better world of innocent late Victorian snobbery, gentle wit and assured charm – wallabies skipping around Lord Bute's park at Mount Stewart, Papal tiaras and Zouaves in Rome; a tree-hugging lady in Worcestershire – 'You lovely old oak, if only you could speak' reprimanded 'My dear young lady, I am not an oak, I am a beech.' All interspersed with clever line drawings by Peter Anson, author of the brilliant *Fashions in Church Furnishing (1840–1940).* Though he had been dead for over twenty years, Hunter Blair's benevolent Rococo spirit still hovered over the (his) Abbey. There were framed abbatial photographs of him looking plump and grand hanging everywhere and for me this helped to mitigate some of the stomach-tautening present.

It had all started as a noble dream mingling Celtic saints, Jacobite Catholicism and the Victorian Gothic Revival. The Gaelic name of the village, Kilcumein, was that of a saint. Before the Reformation the land at Fort Augustus had belonged to the monks of Beauly which was later the principal estate of the Frazers of Lovat. Bonnie Prince Charlie's chaplain at Culloden had been a Scottish Benedictine monk. For the late-Victorian Catholic romantics like Bute and Lovat and Hunter Blair, Fort Augustus was the ideal site for their dream of a revived Scottish monasticism: Arcadia in the wilderness. The garrison, which during the Napoleonic era had still numbered eighty to a hundred soldiers, had finally departed during the Crimean War, never to return. In 1867 the Fort was bought by Thomas 14th Lord Lovat (he owned most of the surrounding land for miles, indeed the majority of Inverness-shire – about 200,000 acres). He used it as an occasional shooting lodge.

But to his son it seemed perfect for the new abbey which was to recompense God for the monastic lands his family had enjoyed since the sixteenth century, and in 1876 he gave it to the Benedictines for the revival of the English Abbey of SS Adrian and Denis and the Scots Abbey of St James. The former had been suppressed in 1803 and the latter closed in 1862. A survivor of the Ratisbon community, Dom Anselm Robertson, was the link between the old and the revived Abbeys. This genealogy was also expressed in the Fort Augustus Abbey arms which tierced the double-headed eagle of Ratisbon, the lamb of Lamspringe and the stylized three-towered castle of Fort Augustus. The heraldic motto *Pax in Virtute* ('Peace in Strength') emphasised the intended idyll of revived monastic life in the defunct old fortress. The new Abbey also received the compensation monies granted by the Hanoverian and Bavarian governments for the earlier suppression of Lamspringe and Ratisbon, and was a new home for some of their displaced treasures: priceless manuscripts and books, abbatial portraits, a huge carved wooden eagle, altar plate, vestments and the Abbot's gold pectoral cross and mitre. The head of the revived community was to be a mitred Abbot, a Lord Abbot. Fort Augustus was the first post-Reformation Benedictine abbey on the British mainland, elevated to that rank when Ampleforth, Downside and Belmont were still priories.

When it opened in 1878, the Fort had the somewhat relaxed atmosphere of the English Benedictine Congregation with easy-going rules of enclosure and liturgy, claret for dinner and a certain degree of hobnobbing with the world. All this changed in the 1880s in an attempt to revive the true spirit of medieval monasticism more in tune with the contemporary mainline European tradition. Prior Jerome Vaughan was replaced as first full Abbot by Dom Leo Linse, a German monk from the Arch-Abbey of Beuron in Hohenzollern, the then power house of European Benedictine revival with 647 monks in its eight dependencies and its own advanced artistic style and pioneering liturgy of completely chanted services. All this was adopted by Fort Augustus which became a leader in the revival of

Plain Chant under the direction of Dom Gregory Ould. The Fort conformed to the Solesmes rules for Gregorian Chant in 1893. Up to the 1960s it was one of only four places in Britain to celebrate the full liturgy with a daily sung Latin Mass and chanting of all the canonical hours[2] beginning with Matins at 4 am and ending with Compline at night. (The others were Westminster Cathedral, and Downside and Ampleforth Abbeys.) This superbly beautiful Latin liturgy was one of three things for which I am grateful to Fort Augustus, though most of the other boys found it an incomprehensible and irritating bore, and used to pretend to faint during the longueurs of interminable church services, or let off stink bombs.

I was lucky. I was the very last generation to benefit, as the liturgy was destroyed in 1967/8, two years after I left, at the command of the then Abbot-President of the English Benedictine Congregation in wilful and suicidal misunderstanding of the tenets of the Second Vatican Council. Though I love the Benedictines, especially on the Continent, I despair of the wooliness, 'liberalism' and occasional iconoclasm of the English Benedictine Congregation. It seems to me a tragedy that Fort Augustus, with its special tradition, did not declare independence and stand out as a model of liturgical practice in Scotland by sensitively adapting its existing chanted liturgy to the reformed missal, in the way that Solesmes in Northern France has developed the liturgy, or smart London churches, like the Oratory, have done so rewardingly.

This is jumping ahead to the end, but my memories of school, and indeed my feelings at the time, were that I was witnessing the collapse of not just an institution but a wider culture. My generation was the last. The last to be able to marshal a shield of quartered arms, compose a Latin epitaph, read old books for pleasure, value formal manners, or tell the difference between Dec. and Perp. Nobody brought up and educated in this country after the end of the 1960s is the same as us. The unassuming cultural link, which

[2] An early Christian development from Jewish practice, viz: Matins, Lauds, Prime, Terce, Sext, Nones, Vespers, Compline. (Prime was abolished by the Second Vatican Council.)

made me feel at home in the 1890s or 1850s as much as in the present, has been broken.

My own feelings were, of course, exceptionally strong because of the particular circumstances in which I found myself, surrounded by non-academic heartiness, all-embracing compulsory games, outward-bound activities and playing at soldiers, i.e. Gordonstoun with God. It was in many ways deeply unsympathetic but I found the parts that suited me. Freedom flourishes in the cracks of institutions. I wallowed in the 'true tradition' of the place, and grasped at the straws left over from the less philistine founding fathers. That is why I may seem in danger of writing a history of my school, more than describing my own experiences there. The history, though, *was* my experience, and was something that I put together myself, partly from Hunter Blair's scrap books and writings; as the monks, let alone the other boys or the lay masters, were not interested and did not care about it. Naturally their attitude drove me, in juvenile rebellion, to clasp the whole Hunter Bunter aspect of the place to my bosom with unfeigned enthusiasm as an amelioration of less pleasant things, and an antidote to boredom. I was also intrigued to discover what had 'gone wrong'. Why had an institution which began as aristocratic and scholarly, with magnificent libraries and museum-quality collections, become what it was in my time?

The school which opened at Fort Augustus in 1878 was the successor to the Benedictine college for boys from Scottish recusant families founded at the Ratisbon monastery in 1718. The foundation stone of the new school was laid by the Marquess of Ripon, Liberal statesman, Viceroy of India and Catholic convert. In its first decades, the school was largely English and largely grand with a recondite and gentle curriculum (as well as 'most languages living and dead', this included architecture) under Hunter Blair's Head Mastership. The aim was to provide 'for the sons of gentlemen a liberal education'. The community, too, was overwhelmingly recusant or Oxford convert English. Of the choir monks in the 1890s, twelve were English, several German and only two were Scottish:

Fort Augustus: School tower and the fort bastions c. 1878

The Abbey c. 1878 with Telford's Caledonian Canal in foreground

the son of the skipper of the red and black funnelled steamers on Loch Ness – the local transport – and Hunter Blair himself. There were three Weld-Blundells, two Lane Foxes and a Cary Elwes. By the early twentieth century the community had increased to about twenty choir monks and twelve lay brothers, and the Scottish element had increased somewhat. Many of the monks were distinguished scholars or artists, in the Beuron-tradition of pursuing *artes elegantiorum*. Dom Luke Cary Elwes (d. 1944) had studied painting in Paris for fifteen years before becoming a monk. He was a friend of Sargent's and member of the Chelsea Arts Club. He was responsible for the striking neo-Roman murals (inspired by the Catacombs) in the Relic Chapel (the large collection of relics of early Christian saints was a gift from Pope Leo XIII). Dom Odo Weld Blundell made a strong contribution to Scottish archaeology. He excavated many early settlements in the Highlands and was an expert on the local crannogs,[3] as well as founding the Abbey museum. Father Cyril Dieckhoff published the definitive *Pronouncing Dictionary of Gaelic* (1932). Hunter Blair had translated Bellesheim's *History of the Catholic Church in Scotland*, written the biography of *The 3rd Marquess of Bute* (Lothair), and much else, including regular contributions to the *Catholic Times* under the pen-name 'Nestor'.

Never one to blow a muted trumpet, Hunter Bunter described the school under his Head Mastership: 'In the course of a single generation [it] has turned out, to say nothing of so admirable a trio as Lovat (the 16th Lord and founder of the Lovat Scouts) and his two brothers, a remarkable group of distinguished soldiers, merchant princes, eminent churchmen, three judges of the High Court....' The 'eminent churchmen' included two Archbishops: Dom Andrew Macdonald OSB, Archbishop of St Andrews and Edinburgh from 1929 to 1950, and Dom Sir Maurus Caruana, OSB, KBE, Archbishop – Bishop of Malta (1914–43), both of whom were boys and monks, and – in Macdonald's case – Abbot of

---

[3] Artificial inhabited islands in the lochs.

[66]

Fort Augustus in their time. Abbot Macdonald was a cadet of the Macdonalds of Cranachan and wore a tartan mitre.

The school closed for a time in the early 1900s (the remote location was always a practical hindrance) as the monks wished to devote themselves more to scholarship, art and writing according to the Beuron tenets. During the First World War the buildings were used for a military and naval hospital, as attested by a brass plaque in the front hall. The school was re-opened in the 1920s by Abbot Macdonald, with a wider social intake than before, including the 'sons of the professional and commercial classes'. Father Anselm Parker was brought from St Benet's, Oxford to be the Head Master. At first the atmosphere, though less erudite, was still 'gentle' with light discipline by Scottish standards and without compulsory competitive games, just English cricket (first played in the Highlands at Fort Augustus), shinty (an archaic Gaelic ancestor of hockey and the subject of a scholarly book by one of the monks, Dom Ninian Macdonald), and the 'Abbey ball game' (an idiosyncratic scramble for the ball inherited from Ratisbon where more or less everything was allowed *except* kicking).

The decisive change came in about 1930. Between the wars Fort Augustus oversaw two daughter houses in the United States: St Anselm in Washington which she founded and St Gregory at Portsmouth, Rhode Island (taken over from Downside). This was the zenith of the Abbey at Fort Augustus. By 1935, with the two subpriories, it numbered 124 monks, the largest community of the EBC. Some of the young American novices were trained at the abbey, and some of the British monks went backwards and forwards, and this American taint was bad for the late Victorian ethos. Father Alphonsus O'Connell, who came from the United States in 1930, introduced a new note of 'muscular Christianity' into the school where he became the 'boxing instructor and spiritual advisor' to the boys. The old informal games were replaced with a regular regime of compulsory rugby and modern hockey which became the most important points of existence. The Head Master from 1930 to 1938 was not a monk but a First World War naval officer, Commander Gilbert Farie, RN, known as 'The Man'. He was responsible for introducing a draconian system of discipline based on cold fear such as prevailed in naval training ships (and borstals) with savage canings conducted with exquisite courtesy. (You said thank you afterwards.) Though he had taught classics for a time at Rugby, he had also worked on the notorious training ship TS *Mercury* on the River Hamble in Hampshire under C. B. and Beatrice Fry, a ship which resounded to the screams of sadistic floggings.[4] Farie's aim was to produce 'manly and independent boys' but he had no respect for learning. This new Americonaval regime of compulsory sport and flogging, philistine and savage, sat at odds with the artistic, scholarly, Beuron ethos of the Abbey, but it formed the character of the school into my time. My parents were unaware of this, and when they asked the Head Master at a preliminary visit, before I went, whether there was still corporal punishment, the deceptively mild and scholarly young monk (with an Oxford degree in Modern Languages and later an Edinburgh doctorate in History) prevaricated and gave the impression that it was rare, without actually lying. Even in the 1960s, however, he was a keen preserver of the Farie Edwardian naval regime. Our Head Master (who spoke all European languages including Serbo-Croat) had regular swishing sessions on Monday afternoons when he dealt with several boys at a time (often the same abject failures week after week). More generally, punishment was indiscriminately dished out every day after lunch, by house masters with a Scottish tawse strangely called 'the stick'. This was on the hands: three to each, or six to each for more heinous misdeeds. It was possible to get a double twice six. It bruised and hurt horribly, though you could mitigate the effect by placing your hands on a radiator, or rushing downstairs to the basement and holding them under a hot tap. On average, quiet, law-abiding boys like myself only got the stick once or twice a term, usually for serious crimes like not stripping your bed back far enough to air it in

4 See Ronald Morris, *The Captain's Lady* (1985).

the morning, or forgetting to collect your clean laundry from the Linen Room immediately after lunch on the prescribed day.

Fashionable presumptions and attitudes have changed so radically in the last twenty years that I should perhaps stress that what I have just described was, in more moderate rations, typical of many British schools and other institutions in the 1950s and 1960s and not that strange or exceptional. The civilized moderation of the previous Hunter Bunter regime was the odd one out. In the course of the last three centuries of generally advancing tameness, the British deliberately and calculatedly kept alive and nurtured a primeval, male, barbarous streak in all classes as being best suited to the armed services, buccaneering and industrial-imperial life in general. Well-behaved, house-trained boys were not required. Potential anarchy was controlled by periodic doses of extreme physical pain (like electric shocks to rats), but not so much as to extirpate the admired barbarism. This was done in exactly the same way that genuine wild animals, deer, grouse or foxes, were also perpetuated on an over-populated and densely cultivated island by selective protection of habitat and judicious culling for sport. This explains why the young British male, even today, is so much more of a violent, medieval, throw-back than his European, homogenized, social-democratic opposite numbers. Whenever I witness rampaging louts, glass-smashing yobs, vomiting football crowds, my heart swells with native British pride. We are not militarist, but we are warlike.

4

Bell Boy to Librarian

The predominant colour in the winter landscape was slate grey. The mountains and precipices, the waters of the loch and rivers, the mist and sky, the whinstone of the walls, all were grey. The Abbey was set on a midge-infested peninsula between the River Oich and Caledonian Canal to the north, and the River Tarff to the south. This exaggerated the Robinson Crusoe – cut-off and abandoned on an island – feeling at the beginning of term, especially the second term of the year in the dark days after Christmas, which is always the worst. 'Homesick' is too mild a term to describe how one felt before adjusting and settling back into routine life with a peer group of friends. It always took at least a week. I still feel a disturbing angst, even going back to London, when I leave home after a few days of peace and comfort.

The journey north was unforgettable. It felt quite all right until Glasgow, rather in the way that you do not realise immediately that your leg has been shot off by a cannon ball. There were other boys from Cheshire, Lancashire, Cumberland and Westmorland on the train with whom one got on – as they possessed some veneer of English civility – even if they were not all soulmates. Boys from the real South travelled up the East Coast line to Inverness, so we were a clannish North Western group on our train. The horrors started after changing stations from Glasgow Central to Queen Street. The beginning of the West Highland line is not picturesque. Apart from the faces of Scottish boys whom I feared and disliked, the views from the windows were depressing: endless vistas of crumbling black tenements and scrapheaps. This landscape of rust and ashes eventually gave way to mountains and lochs, becoming ever more desolate as the train slowly twisted its way into the setting sun. The vast peat bog of Rannoch Moor was ineffably sad, seemingly uninhabited (though there was a school there somewhere with even tougher Scottish boys; they were Protestant and wore the kilt every day, and were fierce opponents on the rugby field).

The arrival at Spean Bridge station took place under cover of darkness, the platform swept by gusts of icy wind – a hint of sleet – and lit only by the feeble yellow glow of a few oil lamps. We then transferred to MacBrain's buses for the final thirty miles. Speeding over humps and round bends in a sick-making race, they relentlessly delivered their cargo to Doom – the pinnacles and battlements, the towered silhouette, the ice grey stone. The arrival! Even now the remembered smell of school makes my inside contract, a mingling of stale food, warm dusty iron from the radiators, and decomposing apple cores. We always went straight to bed without supper (as we had missed it), even though we had been travelling all day and dinner was not served on the train. A cheerful, informal meal with hot cocoa on arrival the first night might have made a difference, rather than going straight to the gloomy, cheerless dormitory. Sleep, at least, was merciful.

The following day was endlessly tedious. There were trunks to be unpacked (which had already arrived) with their counted pairs of grey socks, white pants and vests identified by Cash's nametapes, 'J. M. Robinson S. B. 121', neatly sewn in by my mother sitting before the fire at home. Then there was the new term's timetable to be arranged with its concatenation of dreary horrors, culminating on Fridays with fish and Army, and handing in pocket money to housemasters. It was doled out at the rate of 2/6d a week and the residue, if any, returned at the end of term. I never spent mine. I never went to the tuck shop. Not for me the easy consolations of boiled sugar and milk chocolate.

The hand-over of cash was necessary because there was nowhere secure or private to keep anything. Pilfering was endemic. Personal possessions were constantly being stolen – soap, pens, ink, rugger shirts – usually when you desperately needed them yourself and of course the blame for the missing articles always fell on the luckless victim. Carelessness and untidiness, boy, lines or the 'stick'. As in the Russian imperial army, it was never officially admitted that there was any thieving at all. This constant violation of one's things caused me more misery than anything else. There was no control over your own life. You were the plaything of heartless fates and the object of arbitrary whims and punishments.

The daily routine for boys began only at 6.45 am (much later than the monks). We got up and plunged down to the basement to get washed in a miasma of dawn light, steam and the faint metallic smell of oil from the central heating boilers. 7.15 Mass (still Latin but 'dialogue' where all the congregation responded) was compulsory every day except Thursdays when we had a short lie in. There was also a lie in on Sundays when we went to High Mass at 11. Breakfast was at 7.45, followed by a punctual visit to the bogs, and equally ritualistic bed-making, before School Assembly at 8.25, a brief epiphany of the Head Master. He said a prayer and made a few announcements including the names of those who had failed their monthly reports and who 'were to come to see him on Monday afternoon'. Lessons began at 8.30 and lasted forty minutes each through the morning (with one small break) until 12.15. Luncheon was at 12.30 after a fierce inspection of hands to make sure that they were clean and free from ink stains. The best way to remove ink, I discovered, was to rub your fingers on the unglazed underside of the wash basins which had the texture of the donkey stones used in Lancashire mill towns for scrubbing the front doorstep, and were remarkably effective cleansers.

Afternoons were blessedly free on non-games days and we were allowed to go for walks (in threes) in the surrounding country. Tea was at 3.45 on weekdays, and 4.15 on Wednesdays and at weekends. There were afternoon lessons at 4 pm on Mondays, Tuesdays, Thursdays and Fridays, and prep began at 5.30. Supper was at 7 pm with House prayers and announcements afterwards, followed by 'classical reading' until bedtime. The country walks and the evening reading periods were, apart from the Latin liturgy, the aspects of the Fort Augustus regime for which I feel a sense of gratitude and I will come back to them, when I have finished the gruesome details of the timetable. Bedtime was 8.30 for juniors and 10 pm for seniors. The younger boys did their prep in the large study halls and slept in dormitories, and only the Vth and VIth forms had their own studies where they worked and slept.

This complicated timetable with its variations from day to day was governed by the banshee shriek of electric bells. They are imprinted on my mind. My first position of any responsibility was school bell boy. You had to remember to switch off the electric bell system on Wednesdays and Saturday nights so as not to wake up the whole place an hour too early and also make other modifications and changes to the system as necessary. This caused me nightmares, not just because I am obsessively conscientious, but because of the dreadful penalties that a culpable mistake might incur. My predecessor, one of the MacSomethings, had forgotten and woken the school an hour early on a Sunday morning. The furious Head Master summoned him, flicked up his kilt and swished him until he cried. That had 100% deterrence value for me. Some people say corporal punishment was not a deterrent. Really?

One Wednesday night I woke with a terrible shock in the small hours and remembered that I had not changed the bell-time for the following morning. I lay there in a sweat. All the possibilities seemed equally horrendous. If I did nothing and it went off early, I would be caned. If I got up and went downstairs I would be caned, even more severely, as there were the strictest injunctions against wandering round at night. In the end, a carefully balanced calculation showed that if I did nothing and the bell rang at the wrong time I would *certainly* be caned. If I got up and dealt with it, there was the remote chance that nobody would catch me and I *might* therefore not be caned. So I crept down in the dark, undetected, switched the bloody thing off, and got safely back to bed again.

The relief! The fates or God might, I felt, actually be on my side after all, and this was a consolation and source of confidence. Otherwise I had little self-confidence or even self-respect. When I was depressed it seemed that I had nothing but a mind and that only allowed me to appreciate more clearly the misery of my condition. But as time passed the iron timetable seemed less of a strait jacket; one was able to mitigate it, even gild it a bit with eagerly anticipated glimpses of happiness.

In the fifteen minutes before lunch, I used to talk everyday to old Father John Lane Fox on his morning constitutional. He was a survivor of the old Abbey and had been at the school before the turn of the twentieth century. He could remember the lime avenue along the front drive being planted. He was my oldest friend in every sense. Even after I left school, I corresponded regularly with him until he died in the 1970s, well into his nineties. I also used to serve his morning Mass whenever I could, rather than going to the dreary School Mass. His Latin was beautifully enunciated in a Victorian Catholic way, and he said Mass with a moving reverence, always at the Lady Altar with its Madonna painting in an elaborate gilt Florentine frame, and malachite and ivory crucifix. My only moment of anxiety was at the Consecration when he genuflected, I tinkled a little silver bell, and his old bones cracked loudly, making me wonder whether he would ever get up again and what I would do if he did not. The advantage of serving Mass for one of the monks in the morning was that you got a cooked breakfast with bacon and egg, rather than just porridge and bread and marmalade like the herd. Not that the food was unwholesome. It was good plain fare. The home-made bread was excellent and I put on weight after the vagaries of home. There were some horrid dishes though. A sausage stew which we christened 'botulism', and dense cylindrical steamed puddings, 'Oh God! Not torpedoes *again*.'

At our conspiratorial pre-prandial chats, there was always a whiff of wine on Father John's breath. He was allowed a daily bottle of claret for his health by the doctor, and also the Rule of St Benedict which allows a pint of wine a day. Like several of the older monks he had served as a chaplain during the First World War and had an army pension and a Military Cross. We used to joke that the pensions of these brave old men were an important part of the Abbey's income and that the Abbot, therefore, had a vested interest in keeping them alive forever. Father John had suffered serious injuries from an accident in France. He served as chaplain with the Irish Guards on the Western Front and one day in 1916 he was talking to Lord Desmond FitzGerald who was demonstrating to his men how to throw a grenade. 'Would you like to try, Padre?', he asked, and passed a grenade, as one might a cigar. It was defective and exploded before the pin could be pulled, killing Major FitzGerald and the soldiers he was instructing. Father John, having been educated at Fort Augustus, we liked to joke, was made of iron: he lost some fingers and one of his eyes but survived. He had a glass eye as a result which was a source of huge fascination. When younger, and bored or tired at social occasions, he would take it out, *ssshhluck*, and put it on the table. He had several spares as he was in the habit of dropping them down the plug-hole when he was in the bath. Passers-by would hear a loud roar. 'Dammit. I've lost my eye down the drain again.' He had been incredibly brave in the trenches, rescuing the wounded under machine-gun fire and burying the dead, and was idolized by his regiment. Some of his exploits are described in a chapter of the soldier-author Patrick MacGill's *Great Push* about the Battle of Loos in 1915 where there were 50,000 British casualties.

He was a true hero to me and I loved this dear old man. He had a wonderful sense of humour and could be gloriously acerbic and irreverent about some of the idiot masters, and even his fellow monks. He enthralled me with stories from the past. As schoolboys they had tin saucer baths in the dormitories for washing and had used them in the afternoon as coracles to skim down the rapids of the River Tarff at the bottom of the grounds. His father, an eldest son, was heir to wonderful Queen Anne Bramham Park in Yorkshire, but had been disinherited when he became a Catholic and married a Weld-Blundell. The old family butler never acknowledged this, and whenever George went home, the butler always placed the port in front of him after dinner and not at the head of the table before his younger brother who had become the squire in his place. This vignette of noble sacrifice always made me want to cry. It was like the subject of a Victorian academic painting.

Within the strait-jacket there was a surprising degree of freedom. Afternoon walks were unsupervised. You had to go in groups of three, in case you were gored by a bull, or fell over a precipice; somebody could stay with you to staunch the blood and assuage your groans while the other went back for help. Otherwise you were free to wander where you wanted in the country, so long as you were home for tea. We talked and talked about every subject, books, politics, music, families, the meaning of new words we had looked up in the dictionary, war, sex, ghosts, martyrs... These chatty walks were more of an education than formal school lessons, and better exercise than games. There were several favourite destinations, one being the haunted ruins of wicked Aleister Crowley's house. It was officially out of bounds, but we explored the frightening, gloomy, collapsing rooms of Satan's chum none the less. I filched a little rhododendron from the garden and took it home. It turned out to be a *ponticum* and has subsequently rampaged through the garden at Hill Top, the devil's shrub.

Another objective was the Battery Rock, a gorse-covered crag jutting into Loch Ness and with the best views of the Abbey. There the Jacobites had mounted their guns and successfully bombarded the fort in 1745. One afternoon my friend Andrew MacLaren and I dared each other to climb the cliff. It looked quite easy from below with lots of ledges and bushes. All went well until I was half way up. Then with sudden panic I found I was stuck. The drop below was vertiginous: a flash of bodies bouncing from ledge to ledge into the depths of the loch passed through my mind. Above, the stone looked sheer as plate glass, and there were no more hand-holds. I could not go up, nor down. What to do? Should I cling to a gorse bush and send back for the Abbey fire engine to come to the rescue? The thought of the embarrassment and awful repercussions was too much to contemplate, and I suddenly discovered reserves of mountain goat; I prayed frantically to Our Lady, and without looking down again I scrambled up to the top, and lay there gasping on the grass listening to my heart going pumpity, pumpity, pump.

Sometimes the younger monks came with us. Father Aidan

Duggan was the novice master and a sympathetic soul. He and his newly ordained brother, Father Fabian, came from Australia and still had a faint Aussie twang. He was a fervent believer in ghosts and the spiritual powers of the Gaelic-speaking Highlanders: their second sight and power to curse. (I always thought the Head Master should have heeded this when caning stupid Macs from the Outer Isles.) He was also a water diviner. I am sceptical about ghosts, and give weirdo Gaels a wide berth, but I can vouch for the water divining. When we tried ourselves, with Y-shaped hazel sticks, nothing happened. But when he held his, the twig always dipped down violently to the water source. He let us hold it with him, our hands under his hands, and thumbs on the ends of the twig, and it did work. Magic? You felt this sudden electric surge and the strong pull of the hazel downwards even when Father Aidan was trying to hold it straight. He also let us try inhaling snuff. The monks used to take snuff all the time, even in choir, which we thought a disgusting habit. Father Aidan's pinches of snuff caused nose-bleeding sneezes in my case. I was always having nose-bleeds at school, especially at exam times; it must have been an inner stress mechanism or safety valve.

When walking palled, Andrew MacLaren, one summer term, ordered a kit by post and we built ourselves a canoe in the carpenter's shop – one of a colony of pre-war sheds, out of sight, south of the church. We then spent our afternoons happily paddling along Telford's Caledonian Canal which was perfect with its smooth, still surface and wonderful views of the surrounding landscape. In some ways it seems odd that we were given such freedom. We could have drowned ourselves. (I love the large signs in public parks whenever there is a six-inch deep lily pond, saying 'You can drown in water.') This contrast between very strict discipline and iron timetables on the one hand and complete, dangerous freedom at other times was, I think, a major characteristic of the *ancien régime* British system. It was typified by NCOs in the Army, the rural police forces or old-fashioned college porters at Oxford and Cambridge who knew when to turn a blind eye and when to be 'firm'. The aim, at its best, was I suppose to impose deference and social civility but also to promote independence, self-reliance and initiative. I cannot say whether it turned out fully-rounded human beings in general or schizophrenics, as my heredity predisposed me towards the latter without outside help.

The extreme example of the genre at Fort Augustus was the 'three-weekly' holiday. Roughly every three weeks, if there was a fine day, the Head Master would announce at Assembly that there would be no lessons today and that we were free to go to the hills for a 'picnic'. This holiday was an addition to the great feast days of the Catholic year – All Saints, Immaculate Conception, St Benedict etc. – when we spent all morning in church attending a pontifical High Mass followed by a good lunch, so only went out for an extended but gentle walk in the afternoon. The three-weekly was a Victorian day-long expedition, partly a treat and partly an endurance test. It was astonishing that it had survived at all into the 1960s, as the mortality rate was high. The year before I arrived, a star pupil at the school had fallen off the cliff at Glen Doe into the loch on a three-weekly and been killed. His memory was spoken of in hushed tones. He had been buried in the Monks' Cemetery, and his neat exercise books had been kept as exemplary relics. Even in my time, one of the lay brothers, Brother Malachy, had been cut off by a sudden mist on the Corrieyairack Pass. His skeleton was found six months later, identifiable from the remains of his habit and his glasses.

As soon as we had changed into jeans, or combat kit or whatever, we rushed to the village and stocked up with Heinz beans, sausages, biscuits and fizzy drinks, as well as meths or gas cylinders for the primus stoves. Then off we went into the hills, in a state of high excitement, let off the leash, like baying hounds from the kennels. My favourite destination was Lady Falls on the Tarff, a picturesque spot near Cullachy along the lower reaches of the Corrieyairack Pass. I built a part-subterranean den of branches, heather and moss which may still be there, as it was colonised by later generations of boys who kept it in repair. It was big enough for three to crawl into. Much of the day was spent lighting bonfires and keeping them going, no small feat in the damp. In summer we went to a little loch at the top of Glen Doe where we swam and sometimes fished. If you caught a trout, it would be cooked for your breakfast, a good way of eking out the rations. I have never fished since.

It was not made clear where the boundaries of behaviour lay. That may have been the point. We just got on with it, each in our different ways. I suppose the younger boys must have gone in larger groups with supervisors. The bigger boys went wherever they wanted in the usual threes. I recall a boy killing a sheep, cutting its throat with his jackknife. He then expertly skinned, cleaned and butchered it, cooking part on a bonfire for lunch. A butchered sheep only has two legs, the others are shoulders. He took the fleece back to school and cured it in the basement ablutions place. The basement was always full of dead feathered things and drying skins, all his handiwork, and he lurked there, fingering a selection of deadly blades. I suppose he was a budding naturalist, or perhaps just a psychopathic killer? A group of other boys, colonials I think from Rhodesia and Kenya, celebrated the end of one three-weekly by burning down a small farm house. It was empty, and they threw their still half-full gas cylinders like bombs through the windows. A shepherd the next morning discovered a gutted shell with blackened walls, as if the Duke of Cumberland had just marched past. The landowner who, out of a misplaced sense of *noblesse oblige*, let the school ramble freely all over his acres and fish for trout in his streams and lochs made a surprisingly restrained complaint to the Head Master. Presumably he was insured. The culprits owned up, and the usual repercussions followed – very well deserved in this instance – but nobody was expelled. The Fort Augustus code was a mystery to me. Some boys who had a reasonably harmless mock-fight throwing eggs at each other on the bus to Invermoriston were treated just as savagely as the arsonists. I think the bus 'crime' was seen as a public display of bad manners in front of the 'lower orders' and therefore in the depths of reprehensible behaviour, while the former was a private matter between gentlemen, and could be treated as such.

Though half the boys appeared to me to be the most frightful thugs (especially the Glasgwegians), with legs and heads made of telegraph-poles, the official line was that we were all 'Catholics and gentlemen, and don't forget it'. The Mac-telegraph-poles were destined in due course for the colonial police in Malaya or Hong Kong, or the Black Watch and other Scottish regiments. They probably all turned out splendid heroes in their chosen spheres. Like many Catholic establishments the school had something of a military tradition. We 'Romans' were demonstrative in our loyalty to the Crown, as well as to the Pope, just in case some snide 'Prot' queried our patriotism. After Mass we sang '*Domine Salvam Fac Reginam Nostram Elizabeth*' every Sunday. Despite its comparatively small size, the school had lost many old boys in the Boer War and First World War as well as in the Second. They were commemorated by an impressively simple Balmoral granite monolith near the top of the South Drive: 'In memory of our old boys of the Abbey School killed in the wars. RIP. Remember them at the altar.' (I do) There was also a war memorial chapel in the church with a plasticine-like carved and painted reredos, work of the monks of Pluscarden. The deerskin baldachino over the tabernacle in the Blessed Sacrament chapel was a memorial to members of the Lovat family killed in the First World War. So the sound of distant trumpets echoed down the cloisters.

The contemporary manifestation of militarism was less elegiac. There was a flourishing (and compulsory) Combined Cadet Force with a naval section on the loch and a boat called the *Narwhal*, an Army section, and a majestic kilted pipe band. I loathed playing at soldiers. It mainly took place on Friday afternoons and was one of the contributory factors which ensured that Fridays were the worst days of the week – the worst lessons, the worst food *and* bloody Army. I hated blancoing kit, stripping rifles, and drill. 'Today we will have naming of parts.' Exercises were equally horrible. A typical diary entry reads: 'Army the worst ever. We had to cross the

Blessed Sacrament Chapel with deerskin baldachino. Drawing Peter Anson.

cold icy Tarff and then crawled for miles in soaking clothes, and found the wrong enemy.' Because I was nearly always top of my form and as our troops were marshalled in order of academic seniority, I was more prominent than I would have wished to be or my military talents would have justified – unable to march in step and bored to death by the whole pointless rigmarole. This had its funny side as the hard-bitten NCOs from Highland regiments who were dragooned in to train us were completely fazed by me. They did not understand the school hierarchy and mores (it would have taken a genius combining rare Freudian insights and historical skills to do that). They were used to uncomplicated, smart, keen volunteers, not reluctant conscripts, and they could not understand what a ridiculous, affected, little English drip like me was doing on the parade ground at all.

To do them justice, the Mac-telegraph-poles were quite protective and often took the strain. They understood the score, and some of them were decent at heart. I think they regarded a small (I was the second smallest boy in school until I was sixteen, and the other was a midget), clever, Sassenach aesthete as strange enough to be treated as a kind of mascot. In the end my general hopelessness – dropping balls, coming last in races and marching out of step – became a good-humoured joke. Besides, they owed me a debt. Once at the end of a lesson some of the Macs were shouting and creating an anarchic racket during a supposedly silent period, when one of the Pots came in and asked who was talking. Sudden silence. Nobody owned up. 'Right. You can *all* go to your house master. The stick – the whole class.' This was my first experience of 'the stick' and being of a nervous disposition I went and got it over and done with as quickly as possible. The house master took a dim view. Twice six. And, I was *innocent*. I had not been throwing things around and shouting. The Macs put it off until the next day. When they discovered that I had already had mine, they hatched a plot and said 'Now you've had the stick and are all right, why don't you go to the Pots and pretend to own up after all. Say it was you, and they will let the others off.' So I did. Self-martyrdom comes too easily to adolescent Catholics. It went *almost* according to plan. The Pots let the rest of the class off, but said to me 'You should have owned up yesterday. Disgraceful. Stick again for not owning up. Go to your house master. Now.' So I got a second (albeit gentler) dose. 'Thank you very much.'

The Army was preparing us for something called the 'Cert A Part 2', the possession of which automatically, we were led to believe, made us a general at least when the Third World War broke out, or when we were drafted to Vietnam by President Johnson and Mr Wilson.[5] The tests were to take place at Fort George, the largest and best preserved of all the eighteenth-century Hanoverian forts, on the shore of the Moray Firth. It is now a historic monument open to the public, but was then a working military establishment, the depot of the Seaforth Highlanders. The prospect threw a black pall over existence for weeks before. I was dreading it: arms drill, and crawling around in the mud, and orientating maps using my watch and the sun. There was to be a complete weekend of it. Hell!

The dreadful Saturday came round. I loved the whole two days and never wanted to leave. We had a marvellous time. Fort George was a Georgian set-piece with handsome stone buildings by Adam, gilded royal arms, a drawbridge and spectacular bastions, sentry boxes and ravelins. We spent the dusk patrolling the wall walks in our uniforms and waterproof capes pretending to be Georgian sentries, gazing out into the misty firth where the Royal Navy sailed, under the command of Admirals St Vincent, Duncan or Nelson himself. The barracks were warm and comfortable, the food copious and delicious, with huge cooked breakfasts, all geared up for choosy volunteers who had to be kept happy, unlike us. The officers who did the examining were a sophisticated laid-back contrast to the over-keen, bad-tempered Scots types we were used to. When it came to orientating my map by the sun and I had finished my pre-rehearsed gush, the charming, handsome young

[5] However Harold Wilson, to the indelible glory of his memory, actually refused to do a Blair and stayed out of Vietnam.

major drawled, 'And what would you do in a fog?' I caught his eye and we both burst out laughing. I passed! To this day I have my Cert A Part 2 signed by Major General The Earl Cathcart, DSO, MC.

We did, of course, serve the Pope too. First John XXIII and then Paul VI. Pope Paul VI had actually been to Fort Augustus for some reason as a young bishop or monsignor and used to send special Papal blessings and indulgences on high days and feast days, or intricately painted and decorated candles for the Paschal Candle-stick at Easter, a special Papal mark of esteem. The church at Fort Augustus was one of the largest Catholic churches in Scotland, and comprised three principal architectural phases. It had been begun in the 1890s to the design of P. P. Pugin (the great A.W.N.'s youngest son) but only the St Andrew Chapel (later War Memorial) and the Blessed Sacrament Chapel had been completed before the money ran out. When Hunter Bunter became Abbot in 1913 he had turned against Gothic and called in Reginald Fairlie (a pupil of Lorimer's and by far the best Scottish Catholic architect) to continue in the Romanesque style. The choir was completed with round arches, a hammerbeam roof and American walnut stalls, and was the best part architecturally. Finally the nave was built to a revised design of Fairley's at Oswald Eaves's behest in the 1950s on the model of a German hall church with soaring octagonal stone columns, inspired, I suspect, by the Abbey church at Lamspringe though I have never seen this similarity remarked on in print.

This was the setting for our worship. We went to High Mass and Vespers on Sunday, and on the great feasts when the Abbot pontif-icated at Mass, vesting ceremonially at a faldstool in front of the high altar in tunicle, chasuble and gremial, mitre, gloves and crozier, before being conducted to his throne flanked by deacons of the throne, in addition to the Mass deacon and sub-deacon, all clad in a terrific set of antique cloth of gold vestments. These had been acquired for the Abbey in London, just as a fashionable dealer was about to cut them up for cushion covers. I have heard this story a lot and suspect it was the regular ploy whenever a clerical aesthete

The Abbey church under construction, 1890

entered antique shops *circa* 1893, rather like the Meissen dish and
the kitten. (Do you know the story? Antique shop. Not much in it.
On the floor a kitten drinking out of a Meissen saucer. Customer,
'Oh what a pretty kitten, can I have it?' Antique dealer, 'Yes'. 'And
the dish with its milk?' 'Oh, that is £3,000.')

We sang Gregorian chant at Mass and Vespers, the boys' trebles
and tenors in the nave alternating with the monks in the choir. On
high days we did some polyphony too, motets or whole Masses:
Tallis, Byrd and Palestrina. We were surprisingly good and it was a
staggering experience. Vespers was an especially beautiful service.
On solemn occasions we processed afterwards through the cloisters
preceded by crucifer, acolytes, and *two* thurifers. (I remember
somebody asking 'Why two?') At the Cloisters Lady Altar we knelt
on the encaustic tiles and sang the Litany of Loreto, echoing down
the vaults and through the 'courts of arches'.

The Vespers chant is among the oldest music of the Church and
goes back to evening prayers of the early Christians in Rome. (The
oldest plainchant is probably the Gospel tone which is supposed to
be a survival of the chant in the Temple at Jerusalem.) Whatever

[85]

their origins the Vespers chants are one of the beauties of life, like grass seed in June, and bring tears to my eyes. On the rare occasions when I am in London on a Sunday, I sometimes go to Vespers at Westminster Cathedral and sit behind a column listening to the trebles and men's voices alternating the Latin psalms culminating in the polyphonic Magnificat. It is unbearable. The emotions and memories evoked are too complex to express. *Sunt Lacrimae Rerum*.

Apart from the liturgy, the truly admirable thing about Fort Augustus was the libraries. They enabled me to build on the book-ish foundations established by my parents at home. Every evening we had what was called 'classical reading', choosing the books ourselves from the library. This excluded thrillers and science fiction but included the whole canon of English literature from the eighteenth century to the present day. Over the years I read every-thing: the complete works of Jane Austen, Fielding and Smollett, Dickens and all John Buchan, much of Thackeray, Sir Walter Scott, Trollope, Kipling, H. G. Wells and Siegfried Sassoon. It goes with-out saying that of course Evelyn Waugh and Graham Greene were firm favourites. But we also read Muriel Spark, Angus Wilson and other (then) contemporary novelists and even 'difficult' stuff like James Joyce and Virginia Woolf. I still think *To The Lighthouse* is one of the dreariest books I have ever read, but I persevered. All this was entirely aside from the curriculum and the books we were studying in class or prep for English Literature O levels and other exams. Access to good libraries, free choice of books, and a peace-ful half or three quarters of an hour every night for such reading was of incalculable benefit to me.

The library was my home. It was a thriving place, and extremely good for a school library. A team of boys acted as library assistants under the direction of a young monk, Dom Robert MacKenzie, who had been recently ordained and just came back from his stud-ies at the University of Louvain (where all the lectures were still given in Latin). He took me under his wing and made me an assis-tant and we became good friends. The librarians' room, off the school library, was a haven. There I, and a group of the like-minded, could escape and sit unharassed on the radiators (away from 'You will get piles, boy'). We even kept an illicit still where we brewed some sort of hooch. We supplemented our book purchase grant in various enterprising ways, such as a raffle, with the boys selling tickets to their family and friends in the holidays, while I solicited free bottles from Highland distilleries for the prizes. They were encouragingly generous. We also catalogued the books, supervised acquisitions, and looked after the newspapers and weeklies which included *Country Life*, my secret drug. I drooled over the articles on country houses, and developed my visual tastes and architectural knowledge at one remove, through the distant tutorship (so to speak) of Christopher Hussey, the architectural editor and a genius. The thrill of these articles and the visual excitement of old architecture was so powerful that gradually in the dormitory or later my study I found houses and architecture more powerful than sex and preferred lying half awake thinking of medieval churches or Chatsworth. Cyril Connolly once said he preferred cold soup to sex. I prefer buildings. I became an architectural historian in the library at Fort Augustus, self-taught, following my own bent and outside any official curriculum.

There was also the Monks' Library, the heart of the 'old' Hunter Bunter Fort Augustus. Officially it was for the use of the choir monks. Lay brothers and schoolboys were kept at arm's length generally, but Father Robert took me and a few others for quiet afternoons browsing there. It was a major library and filled most of the ground floor of the monastery block (the eighteenth century barrack rooms of the Hanoverian Fort) which had been connected by pointed Gothic arches inserted by J. A. Hansom in the 1870s. Tall traceried Gothic windows faced over the lawns and the loch and the magnificent mountain and forest-framed view to infinity.

Gothic pitch pine bookcases contained about 50,000 volumes and there were Victorian folio cabinets and glass-topped display cases full of intriguing treasures. Holland blinds in the windows protected the bindings from the harmful effects of sunlight and there was still the original Victorian linoleum with patterned borders on the floor, carefully polished by the lay brothers. Sitting on the library catalogue was a Chinese porcelain Buddha figure with a nodding head which was a nicely incongruous touch and has stuck in my memory for that reason. All the furniture, including chairs and writing tables, had been designed for the room by P. P. Pugin.

As to be expected in an establishment like Fort Augustus, there was a large theological and philosophy section, with rows of vellum-bound scriptural works, exegeses, tracts and sermons. There was also a comprehensive collection of books on Scottish history, literature, topography, Celtic subjects, Gaelic and Highland lore generally. From bookplates and other clues I soon discovered that the library was not just one library but a series of collections which had been given to the Abbey over the years.

The nucleus of the Abbey collection comprised the manuscripts, archives and special treasures which the Benedictines had brought back to Britain from Germany when expelled in the nineteenth century. The most important treasure of the library came from Ratisbon. This was the *Marianus Codex* dating from 1080 with marginalia in Middle Irish, which is the oldest surviving written Gaelic. (This is now in the National Library of Scotland.) There were also twenty-five incunabula, several of which were brought back from Germany, a Book of Hours which had belonged to Queen Mary of Guise (one of a group of fine books given by Lord Ralph Kerr), an illuminated missal where the reference to Thomas à Becket had been crossed out in red ink by order of Henry VIII.

Another historic collection which formed an important component of the library was the Cassidy or O'Hagan Collection. This was a magnificent assemblage of recusant material including six first editions of the Douai translation of the New Testament. These books were collected by Father Cassidy, an Irish Franciscan, and had been bought by Lord O'Hagan (Lord Chancellor of Ireland) whose nephew was at school at Fort Augustus. Lord O'Hagan, on a visit, had been so impressed with the monastic liturgy and the way in which the boys participated that he entrusted the Cassidy library to the Abbey.

Scottish books made up the third important portion of the library, comprising the Gordon Collection and the Cameron-Head Library. The Gordon Collection was devoted to Celtic and Gaelic material and the early history of Scotland. It was acquired with funds given to the Abbey by Sir Robert Gordon of Letterfourie who had been a student at Ratisbon. The Cameron-Head Library was presented by Mrs Christian Cameron-Head of Inverailort and was devoted to Jacobite history and the Highlands.

The Abbey librarian during my years there was Father Augustine Grene, 'Gussy', a classics scholar, who strove to uphold the civilised standards of an earlier age and lovingly cared for the collections, about which he was knowledgeable. He was also a keen gardener, who maintained the herbaceous border in the cloister garth where he could be seen in the afternoon, dressed in corduroy trousers and busy with his wheelbarrow and spade. Many of the books on the shelves had been specially bound under Hunter Bunter's direction by Maclehose of Glasgow in half vellum, gilt with green labels. He made a point of having the less accessible and less used books on the upper shelves handsomely bound so as to add to the attractive appearance of the library but not to be vulnerable to heavy hands. The sections covering heraldry, art, archaeology and architecture were a particularly happy hunting ground for me. The architectural section contained all sorts of interesting goodies, including a large volume of sixteenth- and seventeenth-century engravings which had belonged to the French Gothic Revival architect Viollet-le-Duc himself.

In VIth Form I became the School Librarian with prefectorial rank as one of the officers of the school, but not an acting prefect. This showed a certain discernment on somebody's part as I was not 'prefect material' and would have been hopeless at discipline. The Mac-telegraph-poles were best left to that, getting their hand in before crossing the world to keep the Natives in order.

5

Georgian

M y 'cultural' awakening came when I was fifteen, at Fort
Augustus, so it may as well have the credit. In that year I
discovered eighteenth-century architecture, contemporary English
literature and twentieth-century music including Prokofiev's piano
concerto, Tippett's Concerto for piano, and Stravinsky's *Rite of
Spring* which were my favourites for a week or two. These musical
enthusiasms were encouraged by Andrew MacLaren, who came
from a more cultivated milieu than my own. He introduced me to
Winnie Ille Pooh, and was a talented musician and actor, as well as
a Socialist *Guardian* reader and pacifist. John Smith and I were
High Tories, and keen aficionados of Peter Simple's column in *The
Daily Telegraph*. Andrew set up the Music Club and borrowed a
clavichord, which I had never heard played before, from one of the
monks (the *other* Father John) and a record player. We listened to
mainly twentieth-century music on Wednesday evenings, all of
which he organized.

Many people come to music via Mozart or Verdi and progress to
'modern' music or back towards polyphony from the eighteenth
and nineteenth centuries. I was the opposite. My musical tastes
began with the Middle Ages, through the liturgy, and then under
Andrew's fierce guidance jumped to the twentieth century. It was
only later that I caught up with everybody else in the middle.
Andrew strongly disapproved of *bel canto* opera, which I now
adore, but I still feel twinges of guilt listening to *Lucia di Lammer-
moor* or *Puritani*, and that, of course, merely adds to the pleasure.

The school orchestra was also revived at this time with Andrew
playing a leading part. Under Father Luke Cary Elwes before the
First World War it had been quite good and had been congratulated
at a touring performance by the Archduke Franz Ferdinand as the

'best playing he had heard outside Vienna'. (This may have been a true compliment, as the Archduke may not have heard any other playing outside Vienna.) Andrew was a violinist (later a professional musician), and used to entertain us on the train home, at the end of term, by improvising Beatles tunes on his fiddle. The journey south was as cheerful as the northern return was mournful. On the way home we always went to the Station Hotel at Glasgow Central and had a huge tea for 5/- with meat sandwiches, chocolate éclairs, cream cakes, currant buns, fruit cake, lemonade and two types of tea. It seemed like the epitome of luxe and plenty: a dream of chrome-plated cakestands, lace doilies and Dralon- upholstered comfort.

My real education came in sideways through the three Ls – the liturgy, landscape and libraries. I had, of course, always been interested in old buildings – medieval parish churches, cathedrals, castles, mullioned and gabled vernacular – but now I discovered 'Architecture' and the Georgians in particular. Apart from *Country Life*, I can attribute it solely to one book: Ralph Dutton's pioneering *The English Country House* (1934), in the Batsford series. To him I owe my discovery of eighteenth-century England. The photograph of Wentworth Woodhouse, intriguingly described as the 'largest of the genus', did it. This was 'love at first sight'. As soon as I was able I was determined to go to see the place. A school friend who came from Clitheroe near me in Lancashire, Christopher Hollis, had passed his driving test and been given a Mini by his father. We filled our hols with architectural jaunts, as he shared my interest in houses and heraldry. The front bumper of his car sported various shields of arms, including his own. After the war, Wentworth Woodhouse, in the heart of the South Yorkshire coalfield, had been leased to a socialist institute of physical education, the Lady Mabel College. I wrote to the Principal. She turned out to be very jolly and encouraging and arranged a date for us to visit. She showed us all over the Flitcroft state rooms in the west range, then used as classrooms and libraries but still with chandeliers, and the huge Stubbs portrait of the racehorse Whistlejacket (now in the

National Gallery) still hung in his eponymous drawing room. The Marble Hall was a gym, with classical gods in niches round the walls.

Then she said, 'Would you like to see the other side of the house?' It was reputed to be as inaccessible as Lhasa. I could hardly believe my luck. She rang the butler. Wentworth Woodhouse was really two large houses back-to-back and the East house was retained by Lord Fitzwilliam as an occasional lodge where he went for a few weeks of the year for Doncaster Races or grouse shooting in the Derbyshire Peak. (His main house was Milton, another Georgian pile, in Northamptonshire.) The family part of Wentworth was still spectacularly furnished: paintings by Stubbs and Reynolds, Athenian Stuart side tables, Rockingham china, classical sculpture and all kinds of wonderful things. Drawers were stuffed with letters from Edmund Burke to his patron the Marquess of Rockingham, and other forgotten treasures. Lady Fitzwilliam had excellent taste and had rearranged the rooms with style and panache, keeping the eighteenth-century wallpapers and old paint. (The college side was all bright, new, gloss emulsion.) The charming old family butler who showed us round with great courtesy and knowledge, in the Holland blind twilight, had worked at Wentworth all his life and knew it inside out. He had a slight limp. His rise through the domestic hierarchy had begun as coal boy before the First World War. His first job in the house had been to keep 365 fires going every day. The limp came from carrying the coal scuttles up and down stairs and through long corridors. Wentworth Woodhouse in the 1960s was a graphic juxtaposition of the two Englands.

Chris and I went on many other architectural jaunts then and in subsequent years. Armed with Peter Fleetwood-Hesketh's *Murray's Architectural Guide to Lancashire*, we embarked on depressing pilgrimages to the sites of the lost houses of South Lancashire like Giacomo Leoni's Lathom and Bold, where though the main blocks had gone forty or fifty years earlier there were still derelict stables, pavilions and rusticated Palladian gate posts scattered around the

Marble chimneypiece salvaged by JMR from Clayton Hall

devastated remains of former landscape parks. At Clayton Hall, the old house of the Catholic Trappes-Lomax family at Clayton-le-Moors near Blackburn, the building was being demolished, but the farmer who owned the site had salvaged one of the Neoclassical white marble chimneypieces and had the broken bits in a chicken shed. He let me have it for 10/- and I stored it in the barn at Hill Top for years. Eventually I passed it on to the National Trust. It was restored by Trevor Proudfoot, and is now installed at Brockhampton House in Herefordshire. But that was about the only significant fragment that I was able to save from the ruination of the Georgian architecture of Lancashire in the 1950s and 1960s. Terrible things were happening or had recently happened all round.

At Woodfold Park, described by Fleetwood-Hesketh as a 'perfect example of late-eighteenth-century design, probably the best and largest now surviving in Lancashire', the brewing Yerburgh family who still owned it had taken off the roof, smashed all the chimneypieces and removed the polished Honduras mahogany doors in order to 'repair the many farm buildings on the estate', though how Georgian joinery could be used for that purpose remains a mystery. We wandered through the gutted shell picking bits of Wyatt plasterwork off the floor, Prince of Wales feathers, anthemion and sprigs of wheat. Even where houses were partly restored, the wrong bits had been demolished. At Huntroyde near Padiham, for instance, the uninteresting Victorianized kitchen wing was converted by the Starkies to the family house in the 1960s while the Georgian main block with excellent rooms almost certainly designed by Carr of York was demolished. At Adlington Hall I picked up from the roadside one of the wings of Horus from the Egyptian gate piers, illustrated in a lithograph in Twycross's *Mansions*. The garden at Hill Top became a museum of architectural fragments.

I joined the Society for the Protection of Ancient Buildings in 1967, the year after I left school, but had started previously to bombard poor Mrs Dance, the indefatigable secretary, with letters about threatened buildings, and in return she often asked me to visit sites that they were concerned about in Lancashire and to send her reports (if my responses can be dignified with so technical a name) about those buildings. Thus from the mid-1960s I lent my feeble efforts to the burgeoning conservation movement which was to become my life's work. It was not until 1968 that the law was changed so that listed building consent had to be obtained to demolish or alter listed buildings. This gave the hitherto feeble postwar listing legislation some teeth, and finally brought the (often completely unnecessary) demolitions under control.

I also became a member of the National Trust and planned summer perambulations round England looking at old buildings with Andrew MacLaren, Chris Hollis and another good schoolfriend John Smith (whose father was Professor of Medicine at St Andrews). Until Chris got his Mini and acted as our not entirely uncomplaining chauffeur, we travelled around by train and bus, staying with friends or relations or, sometimes, in youth hostels.

Chris had an aunt who lived in a nice place at the foot of Box Hill in Surrey, and she kindly used to invite us all to stay. It made a good base for Polesden Lacy and other Surrey houses, and was also convenient for visits to London. Other close schoolfriends lived in Dorset and Derbyshire and their fathers soon found themselves driving me to Chatsworth or Sherborne Abbey.

One of those friends was Gerard Wilberforce, great-grandson of Samuel, Bishop of Oxford and Darwin's opponent. Gerard lived at Purse Caundle House in Dorset and is one of the contemporaries with whom I've remained in regular contact. He later became a priest and Catholic chaplain of Exeter University. I've not tested his Faith by asking him whether he has forgiven Dolly and the other Pots. He was brave and never compromised. Rather than asking the Macs for the vegetables at lunch, he would say disdainfully, 'Please could you pass the substance in the tin dish.' I admired him for that.

The quasi-military planning of these architectural expeditions kept me in a state of happy anticipation while back in Siberia in term-time. My study piled up with Ordnance Survey maps of England and railway timetables. I wrote to Pitkin Pictorials, or direct to the houses, to order guide-books of Wilton, Chatsworth, Ickworth, Woburn, Hatfield or Luton Hoo, so that I was fully briefed ahead of the expedition. Even if one never got there one could visit them vicariously in the mind and pretend one was not still stuck in Inverness-shire. I rather impertinently (and with hind-sight embarrassingly) wrote to the owners making suggestions for rearranging and improving their houses. The Duchess of Devonshire responded saying that she 'agreed entirely' that the display cases of china were incongruous in the Sculpture Gallery but she could not think of anywhere else to put them. The Duke of Bedford, equally politely, wrote back that mine was the only 'sensible letter' he had ever received from a member of the public. What a bore it must have been for them to receive idiotic letters from a schoolboy. How courteous, patient and kind to reply so encouragingly. They can have had no idea how much this correspondence with the Outside World, and the proxy architectural thrills involved, meant to me, stranded in the Northern wastes trying to forget about cricket and Army.

To be fair, I also received encouragement from some of the schoolmasters. Though the Fort was a monastic school and the Head Master and house masters were Benedictines, many of the schoolmasters were lay-men and ranged from aged, incompetent cynics to naïve, enthusiastic, young things filling in straight from university or between jobs. My maths master, Mr Palmer, fell into the former category. I was hopeless at maths but his tutoring did not help. It took me three goes to scrape through Maths 'O' Level, which destroyed any hope of becoming an architect (thank God) because in those days you had to have Maths 'A' level to go to a school of architecture. While he tried to explain the mysteries of algebra or logarithms, I am afraid I was miles away contemplating the even greater mystery of this ancient (I suppose he was in his fifties?) dried up old thing and his wife 'making love'. I had only seen farm animals and dogs at it, and my fifteen-year-old mind boggled at the thought of the Palmer nuptial bed. The whole idea induced the same vertiginous incomprehension as the unknowable vastness of the universe or the antiquity of the stars.

The rapid succession of French masters also came into the 'frightful' category, which is why, though I did French to 'A' level, I cannot speak the language today, only read it. The most colourful was the Baron von Schweitzer from Alsace and looking like the Count d'Orsai or the young Disraeli with black ringlets and green frogged jackets. He had a sneery, slight Germanic tone of voice and an affected manner. He was an irresistible figure of fun to the boys. He had some weird phonetic system for pronouncing French which left us merely bemused. He once sent me out of the class for laughing at him – the laughter of desperation. Standing in the corridor, I was found by the Head Master, as was the intention, who asked me why I was there. When I explained (we were taught to tell the truth) he sent me to my house master. The latter, however, failed to deliver the expected thrashing and merely advised me quite gently not to be 'discourteous to the masters', with a nuance of tone which implied 'even if they are contemptible'. I was not surprised when Schweitzer did not last the course and was cashiered in mid-term.

He was a keen rider and had a white horse. One's retro imagination pictures him in his green frogged semi-Hussars outfit prancing around on a Marengo-type stallion. He once galloped over the sacred turf of the games fields which caused a furore as – unlike me, a farmer's boy – most of the school had not had anti-tetanus jabs. Insult followed injury when he explained airily that he thought they were just ordinary countryside! He also gave some of the pupils riding lessons at the little trekking stables in the village. That was the immediate cause of his downfall. When he thought they were not 'shaping' properly he would give them one or two strokes with his riding crop. This amateur intervention caused outrage for some inexplicable reason. Was he trespassing into a protected cartel? Or was he, unlike all the other floggers of course, thought to be 'kinky'? Whatever the reason, as soon as the news got around he was put on the next train from Inverness to the South. As Kitty, the matron, drove him along the shores of Loch Ness in the school car, he screamed 'Thank God. I never want to see ghastly Loch Lomond again!'

At the other end of the scale we had a succession of inspired history and English masters. The senior history master for many years, Mr Fowles ('Chick' to the boys), was an austere but brilliant pedagogue who instilled in us the important discipline of looking things up for yourself in the library, and also a healthy scepticism about sources. 'Boys. Do not regard a *tax-return* to the King as the true indicator of the economic prosperity of Coventry in the fifteenth century.' Chick was ruthless with the lazy and the failed detritus of his classes formed a substantial portion of the Head Master's Monday afternoon flogging task, but he was perfect for me, pushing me from amateur enthusiast to a proper historian. I was top of his class and won the school history prize more than once as a result. It was almost entirely thanks to his academic rigour that the interests, inherited from my grandfather, developed into something serious and I went on to take a First in medieval history (and two doctorates). It is distastefully un-English perhaps to be so immodest as to mention this, but as I was hopeless at maths, science, rugger and soldiers, there is no point in being ridiculously evasive about one of the few things I could do well.

The other master who helped to transform life was my English master, Mr Anderson – 'Tony' to us, as he looked like the comedian Tony Hancock. Everybody, boys, lay-masters and monks, had nicknames at Fort Augustus except, rather chillingly, the Head Master who was always referred to as Mark, his real name. Tony arrived in our philistine, Spartan, Northern world as an invader from another planet. The effect was like those old vodka adverts: 'shattering'. He was svelte and young (and in due course was to marry the sister of one of the boys). He was an Oxford graduate who had read Greats at Wadham, in Maurice Bowra's time, and he came to us straight from Turkey where he had briefly worked for the BBC World Service. He himself, with an ironic smile, pointed out the parallels with Paul Pennyfeather at Llannaber Castle, and read aloud to us Waugh's *Decline and Fall* on Saturday mornings. He had a good, mellifluous reading voice and held even the Macs spellbound. He was different from the other masters. If he had not been so glossily civilized, he could almost have been one of us, one of the boys.

He went to London to have his hair cut and see his tailor. He wore silk shirts and smelt faintly of manly Trumper's potions, lime flower water or something, and the Balkan Sobranie cigarettes which he smoked. It is difficult to convey how sensational and astonishing this was to us. Now it is almost impossible to eat in a restaurant in London because of the stale-alcohol stink of cheap aftershave wafting from the waiters and wrecking one's taste buds, but I was brought up in a world where men smelt only of Wright's coal-tar soap, and possibly Virginia tobacco. One shaved (when one did) with ordinary soap and washed one's hair ditto. Even shampoo was thought a bit effeminate.

The urbane aura of 'Tony' is what sticks in the mind and made the most immediate impact at the time, but he was also a very good teacher. He introduced us to contemporary English writers such as Iris Murdoch and Anthony Powell (who, to be honest, I have always thought over-rated) and widened our tastes considerably. He disapproved of the term 'classical reading' for our evening lectionary. 'It is just literature, boys.' He disapproved of a lot at Fort Augustus altogether, which we found reassuring. He was appalled by the antique barbarism, especially the beating, and never sent boys to their house masters or the Head Master. He had sympathy and respect for the boys themselves and did his best to open their eyes and ears. He probably had the most impact on Andrew MacLaren, as Tony was himself a good musician and saw the potential there. After he left the Fort he became a lecturer in music at Leeds University. He was the moving force in reviving the school orchestra, and also in the production of the twice-a-year school plays which became more ambitious after his arrival.

I only appeared on the boards once at the Fort – as one of Major Stanley's daughters in *The Pirates of Penzance*. The Wright brothers were the lovers Mabel and Frederick. Henry Steuart Fothringham of Fothringham and Pourie made a splendid Pirate King. All the nicest Scots boys at the Fort seemed to have a variation of Stuart in their name somewhere, like the Johnston-Stewarts of Physgill of which the youngest, Bernard, was my contemporary. He was a keen shot and established the school gun club which met on Saturdays and Wednesdays. In those days, it was perfectly all right for boys to carry shotguns around on trains; now the police would probably imprison you for life.

I suddenly realize that I am inadvertently painting an over-attractive picture of our concentration camp with Andrew establishing an orchestra, Bernard a gun club, and myself wallowing in old libraries, liturgy and architecture. Those were exceptional high points when I was fifteen or sixteen and still, for that reason, stick in the memory. The general reality was grinding tedium and sickening dread, the latter declining and the former increasing with age. By the time I left I was ready to scream with boredom.

I drove everybody mad at home for years after *The Pirates*, going round whistling or singing 'Poor wandering one' to myself. But thereafter I switched to being a stage-hand, painting the scenery, acting not being my thing. I am far too self-conscious. The stage occupied many Saturday afternoons and for the hopeless was even allowed as a substitute for cricket, my least favourite game, as it went on so long. At least rugger and hockey were comparatively short sharp shocks and after a hot shower you could go back to sitting on a radiator and reading a book. Cricket went on all afternoon, and put me off the smell of grass clippings for life. The backstage and green room became another haven, like the librarian's office. One term we did *Amahl and the Night Visitors*, a then popular Christmas operetta by Menotti. Andrew MacLaren was the mother. He usually played all the best women's roles and made a good sinister Lady Macbeth or snooty Lady Teazle.

The stage-hands designed and erected what I remember as our best set for *Amahl*, with a stable thatched in real straw. One of the other hands was Seed Minor (nicknamed, of course, Semen, brother of the youngest monk, Father Benedict, who kept bees and taught physics). The Seeds had a large arable farm in Berwickshire, so like me he was a farmer's son. He, however, knew how to drive a tractor. We just went off to the garage and helped ourselves to the Abbey tractor and zoomed off into the country along the public roads, without any driving licence or a by-your-leave, until we found a farm. The tenant was pleased to give us as much straw as we wanted. We made several journeys back and forth. My heart was in my mouth in case we were caught: I was sure it was a swishing offence. At one point we were overtaken by the monastery bursar, Father Maurus, on his bicycle, taking his large Scottish deerhound for a walk. The monk cycled. The dog lolloped along beside at the same pace. Nothing was ever said. Was it not noticed that we had absconded with the tractor? Or perhaps it was thought to be a splendid example of initiative and a blind eye was taken? At the Fort one never knew. One was punished when one had not broken any rules, and overlooked when one had. Perhaps it all equalled out in the sight of God.

For Sheridan's *School for Scandal* we did a single Georgian room-set which served for all the different houses required with a slight rearrangement of the pictures and furniture. We borrowed some of the Hunter Bunter tables and wig stands from the Hospice. The set was *trompe* panelled and painted in an authentic Georgian green. Tony gave us an amusing tongue-in-cheek review where he mentioned that apple green was obviously so fashionable, that it adorned *every* drawing room in London in 1753. We painted all the canvas flats and backdrops in natural powdered colours and rabbit skin size which we mixed ourselves in large tins, and needed a bath afterwards from splashing each other in magenta and blue, and chrome yellow and cobalt.

I was nearest to balanced equilibrium at the age of fifteen and sixteen, thanks to Chick and Tony, Father John and Father Robert, the stage and the library, and a small group of close friends – Gerard Wilberforce, John Smith, Andrew MacLaren, Chris Hollis, Bernard Johnston-Stewart. Everything began to go wrong when I was seventeen. The monastery was falling to bits. There were sudden changes of bursar – always a sign of financial disaster. Monks being monks, they have never been good at managing money or at business, and the adjoining land and houses in the village had gradually been sold off over the years. Rising inflation, and the drastic deterioration of the British economy from 1963 onwards (reaching nadir in the 1970s) wasted the investment portfolio and wiped out the Abbey's endowment fund. Many of the older monks died or seemed to have 'health' problems, i.e. trouble with drink. Some of the young monks became disenchanted and defected. The Australians, for example, went back to Australia. The Lovat house master, 'Dan', a.k.a. Father Lawrence, doubled as bursar for a time and spent more and more time away in the monastery struggling with intractable problems and becoming ever more addicted to the whisky bottle. He had been house master of Lovat since 1941 and, whatever one might think of his methods and social anthropological outlook, he was largely responsible for an unchanging, rock-like quality in the place.

The revolutions in the faraway outside world – the 'winds of change' in Africa and the end of 'East of Suez,' the 'Swinging Sixties' in London – and the Second Vatican Council in Rome undermined the substructure. There was a change of Head. The good schoolmasters left. By the mid-1960s it was all over: the Industrial Revolution, the British Empire, the Tridentine Roman Church, Fort Augustus Abbey. But we lingered on, increasingly bewildered, half-hearted and sceptical; not yet post-modern. At seventeen I should have asked my parents to take me away and send me to a crammer or something, anywhere. But it never crossed my mind and they were in such a state they could not have made a decision anyway. I was brought up always to finish a book, sit through a dreary film to the worthless end, stick at an unsuccessful marriage. School was a bit of all three, and my imagination and mental machinery were unable to grasp the obvious, and just *leave*. In retrospect, this was an even more disastrous mistake than going to the Fort in the first place.

Home was worse. My grandfather died in January 1965. Unknown to me, he had been ill with cancer of the bowel for some time but nobody had explained, and so his death came as an unexpected, sudden shock to the grandchildren. The Monsignor presided over the last rites. We had Latin prayers for the dead, kneeling at my grandfather's open coffin, surrounded by flowers and lit candles in the dining room at Heaton House, the night before the requiem. Somebody rang the front doorbell in the middle which broke the spell and made my younger sisters giggle. The same rites had happened for my great-grandfather Cotton in 1959, so I can remember seeing two waxy dead bodies of relations as a child. My mother was very good at explaining this. 'They have gone. It is only a doll left here.' Once, in Russia with friends years later, we encountered a group of corpses laid out before the high altar of the Andrew Nevsky Monastery in St Petersburg, ready for a funeral. My companions were shocked. I was the only one who had seen a corpse before, which surprised me.

Some people never recover from the death of their life-partner, like swans. My grandmother was one of those. Though she lingered on into her eighties, she hardly spoke again. Heaton House was sold and wrecked. She made me feel guilty, by reproaching me for not seeing more of my grandfather latterly, in the school holidays. But I was staying with my friends around the country. Nobody had told me he was ill and dying or naturally I would have visited him more often.

Financial affairs at home went from bad to very bad. My father had lost money on the failed farm. A street of little houses – William Street – in Preston which he owned himself was compulsorily purchased for a derisory sum and 'slum-cleared' for a tower block of flats. He had hardly anything coming in. Though my grandfather was comparatively well-off – he had had an income of about £4,000 p.a. in the 1940s – my father had no money. When my grandfather died, my father and his two sisters came into the rents from my grandfather's trust property in Preston and Blackpool – but my grandfather left nothing directly to my father because of his known inability to manage his financial affairs. This did not affect me immediately as my grandfather had set up my own educational trust to pay my school fees (but nothing else). Catcrag Farm and Lunesbridge Farm were bequeathed to my grandmother outright, leading to two lots of death duties. She already owned Hill Foot Farm herself. She had no business acumen and had always depended on my grandfather in such matters. The agent mismanaged her property. When Catcrag finally came to me many, many years later it was in a terrible state, all my grandfather's investment wasted. Even Hill Top was not bequeathed to my father directly, but placed in the family company which, after the warehouse closed, my grandfather had turned into a property-owning vehicle, for tax reasons. My mother minded most about that. She saw herself as being homeless. This was not strictly true, as everything belonged to family trusts or the company in which my father had some interests. Eviction was not a possibility. But it became an obsession and the worries infected everyone.

Out on the farm, the animals died. The hens were not replaced after the fowl pest epidemic and the cabins rotted away, empty and melancholy. A listless, despairing shadow descended.

When I returned for the holidays at the end of term from school, not only had nothing happened while I was away, but the bed had hardly been made up during those long three months of absence. I almost dreaded coming home and facing all this more than going away. My mother resentfully took various small jobs to help pay for the sisters' schooling. She was good at sums and could help with people's accounts. The three sisters (now growing up and much prettier than I) were weekly-boarders at a convent, and so had to face the gloom and chaos at home every weekend as well as the holidays. I certainly found it hard to cope with the way in which my initial joy on homecoming was almost immediately turned to misery. Perhaps this is general adolescent angst? If so, it was exacerbated by circumstances in my particular case. It was the mental rather than the physical aspects of grinding poverty that were difficult. After all, we were quite hardy physically. It was our minds which were sensitive and fragile.

This all sounds like dreary whingeing. It is not. I have never much cared for luxuries, and do not mind having been poor as a teenager. In fact, I am glad of it; it softened my feelings towards others, and made me more thoughtful than I might have been. When I came to work in London in the mid-1970s with the GLC Historic Building Division I was shocked by poor, old women living in cold, dripping attics smelling of cats and damp newspaper in Wilmington Square or Calthorpe Street, or in the East End. It was a wish to help improve their condition, as much as the aesthetic urge, that fuelled my efforts to restore those handsome Georgian terraces. That may make me sound like a zealous Victorian philanthropist, but perhaps you know what I really mean.

The trouble was that this family crisis coincided with my own personal dilemma. I had done quite well in my Oxford and Cambridge Board 'O' levels, apart from maths; even passing Art which was not, of course, on the school curriculum but which I did myself as half the paper comprised architectural history, medieval parish churches to be precise, and that carried me through. The system at Fort Augustus was to do Scottish 'Highers' the year after 'O' levels, and then in the VIth form English 'A' levels for those going to English universities. After my Scottish 'Highers', I applied for and received offers from the Scottish universities, including St Andrews. I then persisted with 'A' levels, including 'S' level history, but lost heart and interest. With home and school circumstances being as they were, and my grandfather dead, I knew that my impoverished parents could not possibly afford a gap year or me hanging around for a further period to do English university entrance exams. So I did not apply for a place in England, and accepted St Andrews. My friend John Smith lived there, his father being part of the university, and I knew and liked the sea-girt medieval town and the surrounding neo-feudal, arable, Fife countryside. I considered myself at this stage to be Scottish by adoption. The decision having been made, I drifted through the last year at Fort Augustus, depressed and bored, loathing the place and impatient to get away and never see it again.

Most of the things I admired there were extra-curricular. There is one thing, however, for which I am academically grateful to the Fort, and that is the school's pronunciation of Latin. There are at least three main English pronunciations of Latin: Legal, English Public School (E.P.S.), and Church or Continental. We spoke a version of the latter which had been adopted as part of the Beuron-influenced reaction of the 1880s. In my prejudiced view this is a much more beautiful form of Latin pronunciation than E.P.S. with its 'w's for 'v's and hard 'c's: 'waynee, weedee, weekee'. In fact I think the two are to each other as Cantonese is to Mandarin Chinese. If you are on a bus in Shaftesbury Avenue and the denizens of Soho's China Town clamber on beside you, jabbering away in cascades of hideous hard consonants and shrieking syllables, you want to stuff your ears to block out the ugly noise. To a lesser extent I feel the same about E.P.S. Latin. The Fort Augustus pronunciation was the same as Continental Latin, not just as used in Italy but across the Continent, from the Balkans to Belgium, and is particularly suited to, say, reading elegiac couplets. Take, for instance, the beautiful poem CI by Catullus which ends 'atque in perpetuum, frater, ave atque vale.' Try reading it aloud to yourself in E.P.S., and then read it, as I would, with soft consonants and long vowels. Which sounds better?

It is difficult to express the effects of spoken words and idiosyncratic pronunciation in print, but they are important to bear in mind. For instance, in the story of Paddy Leigh Fermor capping the captured General Kreipe's quotation from Horace's Ode I. ix: 'Vides ut alta stet nive candidum Soracte ...', on Crete in the Second World War, by reciting the remaining six stanzas, would the German general have realized at first that he was speaking Latin at all? The pronunciation of Heidelberg or Beuron (and presumably, Berlin) is so different from the King's School, Canterbury. The Continental form of Latin pronunciation which I was taught also affects my English. Many Catholics of my generation and education have a particular form of R.P. which is tinctured by their Latin, long vowels, for instance, in English words of Latin derivation and short for some from Greek. There were of course, nearly as many variations of R.P. thirty or forty years ago as there were regional accents – Anglican, Army, Oxford, Catholic and so forth. At one time I could tell whether somebody was, say, a land-agent or not, entirely from their form of pronunciation, though to an outsider all R.P. users presumably sounded the same. Just as I could tell whether people came from Preston, Chorley or Wigan, from the varying roundness of their tones, when to others they must all have sounded 'Lancashire'. This is no longer the case, as the standard modern London accent becomes more and more prevalent, reflecting the economic and cultural predominance of the capital in what has become essentially a single mercantile City state, like the Republic of Venice in the last, shorn centuries. (I think this is a *Good Thing*, by the way, before you get me wrong!)

The summer term – and school life – drew to an end. The Head Master (Mark's successor, the Abbey librarian 'Gussy') gave talks to some of the leavers with worthy advice for the world, like always having enough money in the bank to pay your income tax, and also about sex. For some reason I was not given one of these sex talks. Perhaps he just could not face it with a 'sensitive' boy like me. I was disappointed as I was intrigued to know how this shy, virginal monk would tackle the subject. I remember once a boy (as a dare), in a religious lesson which had got onto sex, asked him: 'What do I do if I get an erection, Father?' Pink with embarrassment, Gussy had responded, in his sing song voice, 'Just say "Not for me" to yourself, and try to think of something else.' Ribald chants of 'Not for me' rang through the windows for days after, and became a sort of code for 'hard-ons' in our schoolboy vocabulary.

I may have been a bit naïve, but as far as I was aware, apart from the fact that we all had dirty young minds, there was little real sexual activity at school. Nobody ever made any attempt to seduce me. On the other side there was a certain amount of ogling the village girls – the 'hairies' as they were called in our chivalrous language – but I think little direct action. Perhaps there were orgies in the laurels but, sadly, I never encountered any. The Victorians would probably have described the place as having a 'good moral tone'. We were truthful and sometimes polite. A modern liberal may assume that such a weird all-male environment must have turned out a 100% poof-rate? In fact most of the denizens of the Fort married conventionally enough, some even 'happily' with now grown-up children. It is one of the unquestioned progressive nostrums, very often peddled by second-rate failed schoolmasters, that single sex schools turn out homosexuals. Why? You might as well claim that they produce people with hereditary heart disease or any other primarily genetic condition. I am not saying that absence of the opposite sex does not turn people to whatever may be to hand, including sheep. I cannot speak for the Welsh, but I am just not convinced that school predetermines sexual proclivities for life, or is seriously character-forming in that way.

My last diary entry for school on Wednesday 20 July 1966 reads 'Terminus. Fini'. And paraphrases Napoleon on leaving the island of Elba: 'Adieu, Fort Augustus. I shall never see you again!'

6

St Andrews

I went up to St Andrews in autumn 1966. The first part of the train journey was the same as to school as far as Carstairs. There the line branched off to Edinburgh, and then across the red-lead-painted Forth Bridge to Fife. The last little branch-line train (now closed) from Leuchars chuffed-chuffed across the famous golf links (which like the university dates from the fifteenth century), with a good view of the medieval skyline: St Rule's tower (an Italian campanile or a stray from San Gimignano), the spires of St Salvator's and Holy Trinity, as well as some Victorian lesser highlights. In distant views the town looked spectacular – a medieval dream – on its clifftop seaside site. Closer to, it was visually attractive as a harmonious townscape. The stone-revetted harbour, scattered with lobster pots, and the three wide main streets radiating from the cathedral ruins – North Street, Market Street and South Street, still part cobbled and tree-lined – looked more like France than anywhere else. Though the plan was medieval the general appearance was Georgian-Victorian with decent stone houses and large pleasant gardens. As the seat of Scotland's oldest university and of the pre-Reformation Cardinal Archbishop primates of Scotland, I always felt, however, that the architecture of St Andrews was disappointing. Everything had been smashed at the Reformation and never thereafter adequately replaced.

There was a contemporary, prim, Scottish respectability that belied the blood-soaked past. The Archbishop's castle, where Cardinal Beaton had been murdered, and the scanty remnants of the once huge cathedral were both uninteresting 'ministry'-maintained ruins with mown grass and over-pointed fragments of old masonry – hardly worth glancing at. The medieval town church, Holy Trinity, was largely a replica, dead as mutton, while the

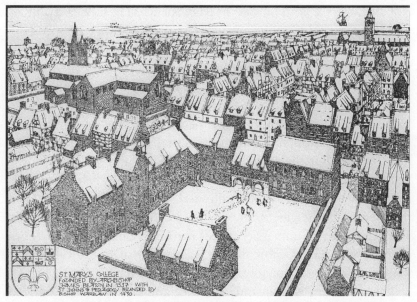

St Andrews: St Mary's College in foreground, St Salvator's beyond

university church of St Salvator had been wrecked by the mob in
the sixteenth, and then so scraped and renewed in the nineteenth
and twentieth centuries as to have little character left. Even Bishop
Kennedy's once spectacular French Flamboyant-Gothic tomb, as
tall as the building, was so mutilated that it was painful to look at.
St Leonard's chapel, with a white-washed interior and candlelight,
was more moving and atmospheric, but had little strictly architectural quality remaining; it looked like a simple, restored barn and
had in fact been truncated and used as a warehouse for some
centuries after the Reformation.

Nor had the university added much in the way of fine building
in later centuries. There was hardly anything by the leading Scottish architects, William Bruce, James Gibbs, the Adams, Playfair or
Hamilton, William Burn, Clyde Young, Rowan Anderson[6] or

---

[6] Though Anderson designed St Andrew's Church (1867) and extended the
Students' Union, and Burn the Madras boys' school (1832) in the town.

Robert Lorimer, John Burnett or Basil Spence. The university buildings were, frankly, second-rate, though the old range of St Mary's
College was picturesque, the former university library a decent
provincial Georgian affair with a good interior, and the main St
Salvator's quadrangle quite seemly in a weak neo-Jacobethan way.
St Andrews could not be compared to Olmütz, let alone Salzburg,
Santiago de Compostela or any other of the prince-bishop/univer-
sity cities of Continental Europe, and that was a grave disappointment to me. But the town was not hideous, and walking on the
Scores, listening to the waves crashing on the rocks below, or looking back from the pier to the silhouette of spires and towers, or in
the evening in the gas-lit, part-vaulted Penns, the past still spoke.
The unique set of university maces made in France in the fifteenth
century with their Gothic filigree, saints and silver gilt tabernacle
work, alone gave a true impression of what once had been.

The university was the oldest in Scotland and had been founded
by Papal Bull in 1410/13 as an offshoot of the University of Paris.
In the Middle Ages, it comprised four colleges: St Salvator's, St
Leonard's, St Mary's and Blackfriars (the latter destroyed by a
Protestant mob in 1559). The Reformation and the disasters of
sixteenth- and seventeenth-century Scottish history – a continuous
tale of bloodshed, iconoclasm, revolution, civil wars, military
defeat and economic failure – had dealt grievous blows, and the
gradual revival from the eighteenth century onwards had taken
different lines from other collegiate universities elsewhere. Rather
than remaining independent residential corporations, the colleges
transmogrified into the university faculties: St Salvator's was the
Arts Faculty, St Mary's Theology, and St Leonard's the Graduate
School. Science is in a modern ghetto on the North Haugh.

I was not certain whether to concentrate on History or English,
my two best subjects. This did not matter, as at St Andrews, like
other Scottish universities, there was a general introductory year in
which you did four subjects before specializing, including either
Moral Philosophy or Logic as a compulsory course. I started out
with Moral Philosophy, English, Modern History and Medieval

History. The last was a new department (1955) under the inspired professorship of Lionel Butler. He had assembled a brilliant young staff from Oxford, Cambridge and London including Jonathan Riley-Smith, the expert on the Crusades, and my own tutor Ann Kettle, fresh from St Hugh's. I had been more of a Modern (eighteenth and nineteenth century) specialist at school for 'O' and 'A' levels. But the Medieval department at St Andrews was so good, and the course so fresh, interesting and stimulating that I opted to specialize in that. This turned out to be one of the *right* decisions in life, and my academic career at St Andrews was thoroughly satisfying, absorbing a new subject through Lionel Butler's *tour-de-force* lectures, and Ann Kettle's and Jonathan Riley-Smith's tutorials, where one read one's essays and was treated with intellectual rigour.

I was a square peg in a square hole in Fife. It was the right place for me at that stage of my development; it gave me the chance to smooth some of the Fort's rougher edges before reverting to being English. I thought of myself when I was eighteen as English and Scottish and so fitted into the particular Anglo-Scottish ethos of the university. St Andrews was an old-fashioned place in the 1960s, academically rigorous but not philistine, with good music, a nice little botanical garden, a full run of back-numbers of *Country Life* in the university library, and a reactionary Catholic chaplaincy run by a Presbyterian-convert who ignored the Vatican Council, and maintained the Tridentine liturgy for the whole time I was there. The pleasant surrounding countryside was easily accessible for walks and architectural jaunts.

In a way it was like the better parts of Fort Augustus without the compulsory games and the thugs or any of the other horrors. It provided a pleasant relief, similar to some people's view of the afterlife: still like Earth but purified of the unpleasant elements. The atmosphere was, perhaps, that of one of the smaller, more conservative Cambridge colleges. It was largely independent/public school, as much as 80% I think, with a large English (50%) and some American (13%) intake, while the Scots boys came from those really excellent schools called Academies – products of the Scottish

Enlightenment – and were much better educated than I. Most significantly St Andrews had a higher proportion of girls than any other university in Britain in the 1960s. It was 50/50 boys and girls, so completely co-ed, like an American college. This had a profound effect on the social life of the place, which was very jolly and civilized with parties and dances ('hops' in St Andrews parlance), mixed classes, and an easy coming and going between the boys' residences like 'Sallies' or 'Regs', and the girls' houses where there always seemed to be tea and buns, or gin. (It seems always in retrospect, though I am reminded it was only at weekends and on Wednesdays).

John Smith, David Wright (Frederick from *The Pirates*) and other boys from the Fort had also come on to St Andrews, while I kept in touch with other old schoolfriends in the holidays, like Gerard Wilberforce, Chris Hollis or Andrew MacLaren who was now at the Northern College of Music in Manchester. This group from school remained my circle of mates. I made no special male student friends at St Andrews. I cannot now remember the name of a single person from Regs (St Regulus Hall), where I lived in my first year, though one had good neighbourly relations with most. The only thing I recall about Regs is that for the first time in my life my bed was made for me. I always made it myself at home and at school. All my new best friends were girls: Patricia Duncan from Wirral, whose larger than life antics kept us amused, Dozmary Boscawen (daughter of the Conservative MP for Wells), Lena Hall, a Londoner, whose father was a Labour peer and chairman of the Post Office (they had a pretty one-storeyed stuccoed Regency house like a folly: Belgrave Cottage, half way between Eaton Square and Belgrave Square), Jackie Rose from Framlingham in Suffolk and Judy Langton-Lockton from Devon, the last two remaining close friends to this day.

Thus St Andrews helped to balance my social acquaintance. Veronica Brinton was my student girlfriend. Veronica's parents lived in Hampshire. One day when I was having lunch with her family there, Veronica and I went to visit Winchester Cathedral. At the west door an elderly couple came out and the man dropped dead of a heart attack at our feet. We rang for an ambulance but it was too late. We got a letter from the widow, thanking us for our help and pointing out that it had been a perfect death for her husband – admiring one of the supreme masterpieces of English architecture and then straight out of this world, with no pain or decrepitude. Something we should all hope for. I have witnessed other perfect deaths. Dining in the Travellers' Club, not that long ago, the chap at the next table dropped his glass of claret in mid joke, slumped forward, and that was that.

Veronica had many cousins in Scotland including Miss Scott-Moncrieff at Elie (one of the picturesque fishing villages on the Fife coast). She was the niece of the translator of *La Recherche du Temps Perdu*. We used to go over there for tea occasionally, and I was fascinated by the Proustian associations and relics such as dried leaves from the garden at Colombey displayed in glass-topped tables in the drawing room. I owed a lot to Veronica's 'tutoring'. I was too callow to give much in return. She was a keen photographer and art historian, and was my introduction to Italian Renaissance painting, having spent her gap before university in Italy and come back a born-again enthusiast for Giotto, Signorelli, Piero della Francesca and Perugino, and their contemporaries in Umbria and Tuscany. Sir Denis Mahon, pioneer of the re-appreciation of Italian *seicento* painting, was her godfather. He and her father had been school contemporaries. On her birthday every year he took Veronica to lunch at the Ritz, and always ordered *sole véronique*. She never divulged she did not care for fish. Personally, I came to prefer Guercino, Guido, Sassoferrato and the Carracci to the *quattrocentro*. At first by her enthusiasm and conversation and then travelling together, Veronica was my introduction to Italy. I remember a wonderful golden day in Rome looking at the smaller early Christian basilicas (we even got into S. Stefano Rotondo), classical frescoes in Nero's Golden House (newly reopened), and lunch in Trastevere, with her as my mentor and guide. This was not just an introduction to Italy and Italian art, but an aesthetic appreciation filtered through a nineteenth- and early-twentieth-century Anglo-American lens.

Thanks to Veronica, I stayed several times in May or September with a New York relation of hers, Ursula Corning (old enough to be her aunt, but a cousin in fact), at Umbertide, midway between Perugia and Gubbio (where St Francis tamed the wolf). The first time I went there was with John Smith with whom I had been back-packing and youth-hostelling in Venice and the North. We got the train, via Bologna, to Perugia and met Veronica there. On other occasions I flew to Milan or Rome and caught the main line train to Torontella on Lake Trasimene, using cheap cut-price student travel which was a huge boon, except that the flights tended to go from Luton Airport, a hellhole and difficult to get to from central London. It was like passing through a very English vision of purgatory to Italian heaven.

There was a nerve-wracking occasion when Veronica and I were due to fly from Luton to Rome, intending to spend the night there and catch the express train to Torontella where her cousin Ursula had arranged to collect us at 3 pm the next day. Unfortunately I got lost on the Underground in the evening rush hour at Oxford Circus, and took us south on the Bakerloo line rather than north. By the time we reached the North London Air Terminal in Swiss Cottage, the bus for the airport had already gone without us and we had to wait for the next. When we finally reached Luton, the plane too had departed into the skies. Veronica burst into tears. Our tickets, like all student tickets, were only valid for that particular flight. There were no other flights to Rome that night, even if we had had the money to pay (I had only scraped enough cash together for the ticket and frugal spending money by slaving for a pittance in one of the new M6 motorway service stations, serving coffee to ungrateful motorists). Veronica was particularly upset, as her cousin already thought her 'impractical and unworldly' and would be furious to drive thirty miles to Torontella only to discover we were not on the train and had made a complete Horlicks of our travel arrangements.

What to do? I found a pleasant, sympathetic airways hostess-type and explained our dilemma: were there *any* other planes to anywhere in Italy, at all? This motherly woman looked at us – we must have presented a pathetic sight with Veronica gently sobbing and myself white with guilt, dejection and anxiety – and said 'Give me your tickets.' She tore them up, scribbled out a chit of some sort, and said 'There's a charter flight for Milan leaving shortly. They have two last-minute vacancies. That way.' I wanted to fling myself at her feet, hug her knees, and chant the Beatitudes: 'Blessed are the poor...' We meekly clutched our bags and Veronica's precious camera, and got on the plane. It was much more comfortable than the student flight and we were given supper on board, and plenty of wine. All for free. We started to cheer up.

In Milan, in the early hours, we went to the station, that vast Axel Haig of a classical behemoth. The chiaroscuro glades of the interior were cackling with life: Italian boys perched like starlings in Birmingham, on all the ledges, plinths and in the aedicules chattering to themselves. Wonder of wonders, there was an early morning train to Florence, and then one to Rome. The latter stopped at Torontella ten minutes earlier than the train from Rome on which we were expected. That gave us just enough time to cross over to the right platform and pretend that nothing had happened. Veronica made me swear not to tell Ursula of our adventure, though I may have overdone the verisimilitude, raving about the 'dawn light over the dome of St. Peter's' and the 'wonderful journey along the Tiber valley'.

Umbria was to me the *beau idéal* of beautiful landscape, in some ways similar to my native habitat, Apennines rather than Pennines, with comparable river valleys and stony uplands, but with sunlight, medieval architecture, food, and 'Great Art' thrown in as well. Civitella Ranieri was that cliché of the travel poster: a *castello* on a hill, encircled by a grove of cypress trees. It was amazingly kind of Ursula to invite all her relations, godchildren, grandchildren of friends, and friends of friends or relations of friends, summer after summer in the 1960s and 1970s for an extended five months of

Civitella Ranieri: photograph by Veronica Brinton

hospitality. She lived on the Upper East Side in New York in the winter and leased the castle from her Italian cousins, the Ranieri Bourbon di Sorbello, in the summer. She was unmarried and had a good income from an American fortune (at her death she left $195,000,000). When her parents died, whom she had looked after and lived with, she was sixty and decided to use her money to restore the castle and keep open house for the young. She eventually bequeathed Civitella to a charitable trust, though she had run it almost as one when she was alive. There was more than a dash of Henry James about the whole generous set-up which, I am afraid, we rather took for granted. There was an excellent old cook, Concetta, who lived across the courtyard. The bailiff and his family also had part of the building. Civitella was more like a little village than a house, and included a church which was a favourite for weddings for the young from Umbertide. On Saturdays there always seemed to be pretty couples, like fashion plates, posing in front of the castle, and the church was always awash with pink gladioli and maidenhair fern. Ursula, who was technically Protestant (and I suspect at least an agnostic), had nevertheless a keen sense of the tradition of the place, and when she first arrived in May every year always had Don Ubaldo, the parish priest from Umbertide, over to bless the castle (more effective than insurance) and stay to lunch. I was there once for this ceremony and we all followed him from floor to floor and round the battlements at a brisk pace as he flicked a little holy water into every room.

Ursula brought her maid Maria with her from New York, who also looked after the guests. All our washing was done for us. There was a succession of butlers in white coat with polished buttons, different every year, local boys and really studying engineering or law, surprisingly beautiful in the Umbrian manner, like angels in a Perugino. One realized that the dreamy madonnas and exquisite saints in the paintings were not idealizations but portraits of real people, just as the improbable pointed hills and pruned trees were not fantasy but the landscape as it was, another art history lesson.

I much prefer Italian food to French. The pasta was freshly made by Concetta every morning, followed by cheese and salad for lunch; and there was grilled meat or fish and a *dolce* for dinner, with limitless local red wine, 'Blood of the Romans', from the Sorbellos' vineyard overlooking Trasimene, where the Baroque eighteenth-century family villa, the Fattoria del Pischiello, was let to the University of Perugia. As it was considered too 'late' to be of interest I was, to my disappointment, never taken to see it.

The guests were an undiscriminating cosmopolitan mix ranging from aged Swiss female relations of Ursula's and other strong-charactered old women – 'steel hands in cotton gloves' as Veronica called them. There were also gay-tie-designers from Manhattan, and large international families with young children, as well as studenty Umbria-and-Art fanatics like ourselves. Ursula was strict about the proprieties and the girls slept in the more comfortable rooms on the *piano nobile*, while the boys shared dormitories in turrets off the battlements. Getting there involved a magic walk with a torch in the warm soft dark along the rose-brick-paved wall-

The 'boys' dormitory' in a turret off the battlements

walks, peering through the open embrasures and machicolations at the lights of Umbertide down below, or listening to the crickets in the cypress grove. The Art squad tended to be the same from year to year. Francis Russell, part New Zealander, then at Christ

Church, Oxford and later at Christie's, was already an expert on Umbrian painting so we christened him 'baby B.B.' (after Bernard Berenson). Peter Marangoni, half-Florentine, half New York, was an architectural student and I think a godson – certainly a favourite – of Ursula's. Jonathan Mennell was a grandson of Lord Vansittart, the pre-war anti-Appeasement principal secretary at the Foreign Office; he was then studying the Sotheby's Fine Art course, and later married a Roman girl. We were subsequently joined in the turret by James Miller, sometime deputy-chairman of Sotheby's.

We spent our days on expeditions to long-forgotten former monasteries, now peasant farms, where we 'discovered' remnants of frescoes in the granary, or a few carved capitals among the drying onions in the former cloisters. We particularly liked dim churches with one fresco, dusty Venetian glass chandeliers and a holy water stoup made out of a Roman altar. We were incurable romantics and this type of nineteenth-century experience made more impact than the massed ranks of carefully conserved gold-ground paintings on white walls in the Umbrian National Gallery in Perugia. Ursula also drove us in her large estate car for longer day-trips. A favourite was through mountain passes and Roman tunnels at Cagli to Urbino in the Marches with its botanical garden, Neoclassical cathedral by Valadier, S. Francesco by Vanvitelli (architect of the palace at Caserta), Egyptian-style theatre and, of course, the Renaissance *palazzo ducale* much embellished with the Garter given to the Duke by Henry VII, or S. Bernadino at the bottom of the hill with the Montefeltro tombs. We also regularly visited Arezzo, Cortona, Siena, and Orvieto for day-trips. We even got as far as the Villa Lante, Bomarzo and Caprarola one year, though Ursula preferred 'early' architecture and old frescoes to gardens, the High Renaissance and Baroque. So in general we concentrated on the former. Neighbouring Gubbio was the special favourite, being a smaller, less touristy version of Assisi or Urbino. It was romantically unrestored and un-chi-chi in those days. A highlight, if you were there at the right moment, was the feast of the local saint San Ubaldo, celebrated with the usual pious synthesis of pagan and Christian; noise, jollity and feasting. The Race of the *Ceri* took place on this day each year, up the zig-zag mountain path to San Ubaldo's basilica at the top where the saint reclined in a glass box on the high altar. The *Ceri* were not candles but three huge, heavy wooden totem poles representing three saints, including San Ubaldo himself. There were three sets of different sizes and three races: for the boys, the youths and the men of the town. S. Ubaldo's won all of them, of course, and had done since time immemorial. Gubbio also possessed a miniature version of the ducal palace at Urbino, for it had once belonged to the Montefeltro, too, in the sixteenth century. It was now tenements and the virtuoso marquetry *studiolo*, almost identical to that at Urbino, had migrated to the Metropolitan Museum in New York; but there was a well-proportioned colonnaded court (with drying washing hung out) which was all the more delightful for being shabby and not generally open to the public.

Sightseeing was a major occupation at Civitella, but not the only one. Sometimes we would just escape to Perugia for the day and sit in the main street, sipping cappuccino and watching the world go by, or laze around at home. There was a reservoir lower down the hill from the castle for irrigating the tobacco (a cash crop pioneered in Umbria by the Sorbello family) and we swam there in the morning, or walked, or just lolled and lounged on deckchairs on the terrace with its view down the Tiber Valley towards Perugia, a vista which was on a par with those from Hill Top or Fort Augustus. Many happy moments were spent there, just chatting, or reading my favourite novel, Stendhal's *Chartreuse de Parme* (in an English translation by Robert Baldick) under the ilex trees, while hens scratched around in the grass and the bailiff's pretty daughter practised the piano in the room above. Her efforts were no doubt faltering and heavy-handed, but transformed by hour and place into music of ineffable poignancy. Those chords echo in the memory.

We had our own music, too, singing Schubert songs round the piano in the Music Room, or playing records on the 'steam-age' gramophone. One year our favourite was the newly discovered music for Napoleon's Coronation composed by Paisiello. We played it over and over and over and over again, until we were begged to stop it. My musical tastes were becoming much less austere away from Andrew's influence. It was at one of the Schubert sessions that a monumentally ponderous German woman confided to us, apropos of nothing, 'None of the angels at Salem smile.' I thought to myself, 'I *bet* they don't.' There was obviously something about one (as Cedric would have said) at that stage, which was a walking affront to serious Continentals and Americans. One of the Democrat-voting New Yorkers said to me at dinner one evening, 'Why are all the young men in England *so* reactionary?' The tone was disapproving. I could only reply, 'I am not typical of young men in England. And they are not.'

Ursula's cousins, the Ranieri Sorbello family, maintained regular contact and were amused by the 'Corning Zoo', as they called us. Roberto Ranieri, who really owned the castle and the estate, used to come over every day to see the bailiff, though I suspect his grasp of his affairs was not all it might have been. Though only in his twenties, plumpness was already setting in. His passion was fast cars. He liked to give the prettier girl-guests a spin in his latest Ferrari, or whatever, along the still unmetalled, gravelly mountainside roads. His mother, Kinka Sorbello, used to come over to lunch occasionally, and consume vast quantities of *grappa*, a fluid which even at my most Italophile I would not have recommended to my closest friend. The Marchesa was a product of the dimmer circles of the Italian nobility, and not exactly Einstein, but she pronounced everything with decisive firmness, from a commanding height. She once told us that all tobacco plants had ten leaves, regardless of their size. Seeing our quizzical expressions, she repeated it, 'Yeez, ten leafs.' We counted when next out in the country; some had sixteen, some six. Ten leaves were a rarity.

As I was going through one of my periodic phases of romantic snobbery – they came and went like the common cold when I was an adolescent – she was all I wanted her to be. Her annual birthday party at Sorbello was the treat of the year. The whole of the

Civitella zoo was summoned to attend and mingle with the Milanese designer-clothes (I cannot remember who was in them), happy crowds of excited, spoilt *bambini* and the mad relations with arms that reached down to the ground and hair like birds' nests.

Sorbello was even larger than Civitella Ranieri, but less pretty. It crowned a conical hill entirely planted with gloomy cypress trees, in the Valle dei Niccone midway between the Tiber Valley and Trasimene. The drive circled the hill for miles, up and up, to the grim Ghibelline battlements, dominated by one taller bell-tower. 'Childe Roland to the Dark Tower came.' It felt like an independent principality and had been one.

The Bourbons di Sorbello were, so they claimed, an illegitimate branch of the main Bourbon family who had come to rest in the Apennines. At their zenith they had been reigning Marchesi of the Holy Roman Empire, occupying a gap in the map between the Grand Dukes of Tuscany and the Papal States. The Ranieri were subjects of the latter, and were Papal counts. Until 1870 they had presented a candle every year to the Pope for their fief. Their battlements were therefore Guelph. We were just tackling the incomprehensible Guelph-Ghibbeline struggles in Medieval History at St Andrews, so it helped to have these two adjacent castles to play with as a teaching aid. (Rather in the way that I think you should be able to have a deer park on the National Health, as an antidote to depression – all those large brown eyes, skipping hooves and little frisky tails.) The Ranieri and the Sorbello family had come together by marriage in the nineteenth century, and Civitella descended through the younger sons, Counts Ranieri, while the Marchese di Sorbello continued to 'reign' at Sorbello, although in our time it was the widowed mother not Roberto's eldest brother who lived there. Hence our party.

We arrived in our cleanest shirts and least crumpled clothes, but still no match for the Italian designer labels, and marched up the huge stone staircase lit by flaming torches to the *piano nobile*. At the top Kinka greeted her guests. Beyond, a vast enfilade of seventeenth-century frescoed galleries and *saloni* led into infinity.

Footmen, hired for the day, in gold epaulettes and white gloves, handed round the drinks and eats; there was always a whole roast *'porcetta'* with an apple in his mouth, which was carved into delicious slices by the most dexterous of the white gloves. It was all home from home.

The *Inglesi* usually ended up playing hide-and-seek round the deserted upper floors, attics and battlements with the younger Sorbelli. Roberto had a slightly dotty but harmless younger brother, Ruggiero, whose idea of fun was to lock those of a nervous disposition into unlit tower rooms and leave them there, until distant faint cries from high places led to their rescue amid peals of happy laughter. My favourite architectural detail at Sorbello was the little Baroque chapel where the carved wooden confessionals had heraldic grilles made up of the family arms in the form of little etched holes (ideal for whispering sins involving *mésalliance*).

Grey, Presbyterian St Andrews, by contrast, lacked such amenities. But I worked hard. Autumn terms were always the busiest, getting to grips with the First Crusade, the Plantagenet Empire and the English wool trade in the fifteenth century, ready for intermediate exams. I never want to sit another exam, but at the time I had a reasonable technique. The best thing, I found, was not necessarily to answer the questions in order, but to start with the only one you felt you could deal with. The most important thing was to start writing *immediately* – on another sheet of paper if necessary – and once the initial ice-block had melted and the brain come out of its panic, to continue with answering the questions, as fast as you could. The poor examiners! Having to try to read all that scrawl, jumbled grammar, misspellings and boring repetitions.

The truly awful thing with an exam is to come out and realize immediately that you have misread a question and given the wrong answer. This happened to me in my finals. As soon as I staggered out of the Examination Hall, I was struck dead with the certainty that I had got hold of the wrong end of a question about the Byzantine army. There were two key elements in the Byzantine army, as you will know, with more or less identical Greek names: one was a hereditary officer class and the other was the ordinary soldiers. I was asked to discuss the importance of the hereditary officer class in the twelfth century but thought it was the other and wrote reams and reams about the wrong subject. Sick misery and dread anticipation filled the months, or was it only weeks, until the letter with my results arrived and put me out of my agony.

At least with exams you did not have to worry about the elegance of the writing. Essays involved a good deal more effort, to construct a proper overall form and flowing sentences. The discipline of absorbing detailed information from different sources, synthesizing it, and writing a short, well-constructed essay was probably the skill taught at university which I most value. Though heaven knows if I have ever learnt to write 'properly.' Woodrow Wyatt once told me that my literary style was a cross between Philip Toynbee and Marjorie Proops.

Much time, especially weekends, at St Andrews was spent out of the town in the surrounding country. East Fife, between the Firths of Tay and Forth, is different from the rest of Scotland, more like Northumberland, Lincolnshire or parts of France with its low hills, rolling fertile landscape, large arable farms and red pantile-roofed villages, especially the postcard fishing villages round the coast. It was largely a landscape of Georgian agricultural improvement with late-eighteenth-century enclosures, shelter belts of mixed trees, and handsome stone-built courtyard farms. They became one of my special interests and, in due course, led to a slim book on the architecture of Georgian model farms (with such a small print-run that it is now a collector's item of considerable rarity). There were also dozens of country houses dating between the seventeenth to the early twentieth centuries, many of which I got to know well. Most of them were still privately lived in. The ancient Scottish families, Lindsays, Bruces, Anstruthers, Wemysses and the rest, had been much augmented in the nineteenth century by newer gentry from Dundee: Nairns, Thompsons and Baxters. I counted about twenty houses in Fife owned by the descendants of jute, linoleum, marmalade and newspapers.

I was a member of the University Archaeological Society, which covered not just old stones but historic buildings in general, under the presidency of the Earl of Crawford, the most civilized man of his generation; he sometimes invited groups over to Balcarres, one of William Burns's best houses of the 1830s, stuffed with important things and with beautiful terraced gardens. The library included the book, stained with blood and water, which Marat had been reading in his bath when Charlotte Corday burst in.

A friend met through the Archaeological Society was Hugh Stuart of Struthers. He had been educated at Fettes but, despite Lord Crawford's encouragement, had not come on to the university. Nevertheless, he attended the archaeological meetings and helped me to organize visits to places of interest. His father, a Fife farmer, was the factor to the Anstruthers of Balkaskie. Sir Ralph Anstruther was mainly in London, where he was Treasurer of the Household to Queen Elizabeth at Clarence House, and Balkaskie was run by his indomitable widowed mother, Madge Anstruther. She was a keen gardener, particularly proud of her tree peonies on the south-facing terraces which were centred exactly on the Bass Rock in the middle of the Firth of Forth. Balkaskie was of some architectural importance as the earliest work of Sir William Bruce, Scotland's first major classical architect. Another seventeenth-century house I got to know well was Melville, designed by James Smith (and possibly Bruce) in the 1690s, for the Earl of Melville, president of the Privy Council. It had been Scotland's equivalent of Ham House. But all the once stupendous contemporary contents had gone; the velvet state bed is now in the Victoria and Albert Museum where it is the star attraction of the English primary galleries. Melville had been sold up, and the park trees felled by a speculator in the 1950s. It was then a boys' prep school run by the brother of one of the Fort Augustus monks, Father Vincent (house master of Vaughan). I used to go over to help when they opened the place occasionally to the public at the weekends. The state rooms still had very fine panelling with fluted Ionic and Corinthian pilasters, coroneted carvings, and marble chimneypieces.

Through Hugh I was able to visit many other places, such as Kilmany, an Edwardian Cape Dutch style house designed by Reginald Fairlie, the architect of the church at Fort Augustus. The cook at Kilmany had started out before the war as a kitchen maid with the Londonderrys at Mount Stewart in Northern Ireland. She told me that all the bedrooms there were called by Castlereagh after the capitals of the great powers at the Congress of Vienna. If she left the basement corridor doors open, complaints would filter down that the smell of cooking was getting into Berlin or St Petersburg. Many of these old family servants in houses were the last of their type, and I valued conversations with them about the 'old days'.

Further afield, we visited Dalkeith Palace on the other side of Edinburgh, another James Smith house, which had been uninhabited since 1910 when the Dukes of Buccleuch, who still owned it and kept an estate office going there, had started to restore Boughton in Northamptonshire and moved there for the summer instead. When we visited in the 1960s, we wandered through the clean but empty rooms with the outline marks of pictures or looking glasses, long ago removed to Drumlanrig or Bowhill, still visible on the walls. Dalkeith has since been converted to offices and spruced up. I think it was on that same February trip that we visited Newhailes near Musselburgh and had tea with Lady Antonia Dalrymple. Newhailes now belongs to the National Trust but was then wondrously decayed and eccentric. It was an unknown and atmospheric private house with all its original contents and Georgian paint schemes. It was the coldest place I have ever been in. It was probably chilly at the best of times, facing north east towards Siberia, but the winter we went, the few radiators in the house had been put out of commission by Lady Antonia's husband, Mark, who fancied himself as a mechanical inventor. The marble tops of Georgian side-tables in the rooms were strewn with the coiling entrails of dismantled wireless sets. He was trying to 'modernize' the radiators by installing heating elements from electric kettles, in the hope that this would be an economical way of warming the water in them. The experiment had not worked. With chattering teeth we gathered round the dining table for tea. The one bar electric fire in the huge Palladian marble chimneypiece, framed with carved swags and flanked by caryatids, was switched off and the kettle plugged in to its place, the only socket in the room.

Apart from the Archaeological Society, my other extra-mural activity at St Andrews was membership of the Preservation Trust, of which I became the student trustee. We campaigned manfully to stop out-of-scale sodium street lighting in the best streets, to restore the surviving small vernacular cottages (always viewed as dangerous, unhealthy slums in North Britain, as opposed to Sussex or Dorset where famous writers or ex-ambassadors fall over each other to live in them), and generally to raise awareness of the architectural beauties of the town. We failed in our two big campaigns against short-sighted developments: the proposed widening of Abbey Street, involving the demolition of a whole group of early-eighteenth-century vernacular houses, and the construction of a huge and hideous golf hotel on the links to the north of the town, which impacted disastrously on the views from that side. Both went ahead in the interests of cars and tourism. St Andrews was permanently diminished by them.

Like most students in the 1960s, I spent part of my vacations doing odd jobs to eke out the finances. This was a more grown-up version of fagging for the Pots at school, and could be equally unpleasant. The worst job was in one of the Forte filling stations on the new M6 motorway, which started out with 'waiter service' of all incongruous things, considering the nature of the food purveyed to the passing motorists. The place seemed to me a shambles, though it had only just opened. The 'managers' wandered around in black coats and striped trousers trying to look in charge. Behind the scenes the kitchen was chaos, with dirty crockery piling up in unwashed heaps like coal in a provincial bath. When somebody asked for a cup of coffee you more or less had to pick out and wash the cup yourself before pouring the coffee in. We were not allowed tips, but I found that if you left a saucer with a few coins in it in a prominent place (when the 'manager' was away 'managing'), it attracted other coins like fishing bait, and I managed to earn more that way than from the official Forte pittance. The experience gave me a life-long sympathy for people in service jobs, especially those with no 'boat waiting outside'.

More congenial were a number of holiday tasks I did for the Lancashire County Planning Office. The aim was to produce maps of the derelict land round the little moorland towns and villages in East Lancashire with their strange names – Oswaldtwistle, Hoddlesden, Haslingden, Bacup, Ramsbottom and Rawtenstall. Developed round cotton mills in the eighteenth and early nineteenth centuries these rain-lashed, blackened stone, hillside places had nevertheless some of the picturesque qualities of Umbrian hill towns, albeit more 'gritty' and derelict. They were completely dead in the 1960s – almost ghost towns. The old industry had mainly closed, though there were still the odd Dickensian family businesses turning out felt, green baize, sheets of tinned copper, or some such esoteric, specialized late-Georgian production line. I used to take my sandwiches, and bus or walk round the streets and the moors all day. On my map I coloured in disused quarries, factory ruins, abandoned mine workings and the like, according them grades of dereliction. The results surprised the planners when I finally completed my task: there was far more derelict land than they had feared. That may be because I had included allotments and people's front gardens in the 'moderately derelict' category. I grew to like these strange, bleak, forlorn settlements with their hard granite sett-paved roads, cinder paths, huge Italianate Congregational or Baptist chapels, Edwardian Art Nouveau public libraries, Commissioners' Gothic Anglican parish churches, Victorian workhouses, well-sited terraces of mill workers' cottages and friendly pubs, all as they were then before architects got to work with cheap and nasty concrete redevelopment. The population was surprisingly nice and pretty for so hard a landscape; many of the girls were blonde, bubbly and always pleasant and helpful. I loved getting lost and asking the way and chatting with them. I never had a single unpleasant experience in these rough-seeming places.

As finals loomed, I started to think of life thereafter. One of the papers was a mini written thesis. Ann Kettle, my tutor, encouraged me to do something on architecture and I wrote a paper on fifteenth-century houses – Haddon, Cothay and Tattershall. This was my first piece of sustained architectural history, though rereading it now, I find it embarrassingly jejune and ignorant. Everybody seemed certain that I should go on to do proper architectural history. They were equally certain that I should go to Oxford. Why not try Oriel where Billy Pantin the medieval historian was also interested in buildings and was a friend of some of the medievalists at St Andrews? This was all arranged for me, and I was offered a place at Oriel without ever setting foot in the college or completing, as far as I can remember, any application form. As it turned out, Billy Pantin was due to retire, so I was advised to ask Howard Colvin at St John's whether he would supervise me instead. I went to Oxford to see him that Easter. He stressed that he would be happy to take me on as his pupil, but that I might find it difficult to get a place at a college. I told him I already had one and that clinched it.

Despite the Byzantine army, I still passed my finals (perhaps they decided that I had shown sufficient knowledge of military arrangements in Constantinople in the twelfth century anyway and turned a blind eye to the fact that I had answered the wrong question). I was offered a research scholarship from St Andrews to go on to Oxford. Only two of us in my year got Firsts in medieval history and both of us went on to Oxford: the other, Peter Edbury (now a Professor) to Christ Church – the whale – and I to the minnow next door, as an eighteenth-century Dean of the House had described these two ancient corporations.

7

Coronation Route of the Emperors

I spent my twenty-first birthday at St Florian in Austria, one of the grandest of all Baroque buildings; so vast and grand that it had summer and winter refectories, as well as an imperial staircase and one of the largest state apartments in Europe. This was part of the most ambitious and also the final architectural tour that I planned and conducted with the old schoolfriends Andrew MacLaren, John Smith, and the much imposed upon Christopher Hollis as driver. The rest of us did a little gentle map-reading as our contribution or made helpful suggestions 'Würzburg is only a hundred miles away, let's go and look at the Residenz.' The Hollis Mini finally packed up in Vienna and we came home by train. The quadruple alliance did not withstand the strain, and Chris and Andrew, in particular, never spoke to each other again afterwards. It was a heroic drive, and thinking back we were not sympathetic enough to our long-suffering chauffeur. John Smith, with his steady, unflappable character, did his best to keep the show on the road, and the world spinning. The aim, more or less, was to follow the coronation routes of the Holy Roman Emperors over several weeks in August/September 1969.

We started with Aachen and finished in Vienna, looking at the major buildings and towns along the Rhine and Danube, and visiting or staying where possible in the imperial monasteries on the way. I wrote (partly in Latin) to the abbots, stressing our Benedictine credentials, and was invited to stay at Beuron, Kremsmünster, St Florian, and Altenburg. Otherwise we spent the night in little hotels, b & bs, youth hostels or sometimes with family friends, when there were any on whom to impose ourselves, and on at least one occasion on benches in the local railway terminal.

We had not foreseen that there would be no petrol filling stations on the motorway through flat, dull Belgium and we ran out of fuel between the Channel and the German border. There was nothing for it but to leave the car on the verge and climb over the fence with a can and, hoping for the best, head off into the country. We found a farm but the owners were surly, unfriendly and unhelpful. Communication was difficult as they did not understand our 'French' so we resorted to a bit of German. Not that we had much German – just some words remembered from Schubert songs. A German vocabulary derived from Schubert tends to be of limited use, as you only know the nouns for watercress, red roses, hedgehogs and other things that do not come up in ordinary conversation. In desperation we reverted to English. This caused sudden wreaths of smiles. 'You are not *German*?' 'No, of course not, British.' Complete transformation. 'Come in. Have something to eat and drink.' Delicious, unknown, Belgian beer was produced, Hoergaarden perhaps. 'Give me your can. I will take it to the local garage and fill it for you. No, no, of course not, I won't accept a penny [what term was the Belgian currency?]. It is my pleasure. British! Splendid!' This was all a massive relief and an instructive insight into recent European history, but it made me sympathetic to the Germans, twenty-four years after the end of the war.

The search for petrol and the Belgian farm-hospitality set back our planned programme considerably, and by the time we reached Aachen (our destination for the first day) everything had closed down including the youth hostel in which we were booked for the night. We were able to savour its amenities the following day. German youth hostels were fearsomely hygienic and clean, and run by SS types who barked orders, and insisted on you folding your blankets at exact right angles and made you do it again if you did not get it perfect the first time. All very different from, say, Dutch youth hostels in which I have also stayed, and which were very relaxed. Nobody got up or washed much, just lolled round on their beds, smoking pot all the time.

Dejectedly we made for Aachen railway station and a degree of shelter. Being German, it was spotlessly clean and you could lie on the floor without succumbing to a contagious disease as you would in Britain. It burst into life at an early hour with happy, efficient workers starting their day, and we were able to get a cup of coffee and a bread roll at about 5 am. We were stunned by the cleanliness, the efficiency, the bright white lights of the German Economic Miracle. Coming from dirty, orange-sodium, declining Socialist Britain, 1960s Aachen with its sleek modern buildings, new industry, well-maintained street paving, fountains and flowers, and overwhelming sense of booming prosperity was a considerable eye-opener. It was a shaming contrast to south Lancashire, central Scotland or Birmingham. We were almost as impressed by all this as by the Carolingian basilica, the real object of our visit.

Having paid our respects to Charlemagne at Aachen, which preserved its medieval votive offerings (including the crown of our Edward IV's queen) and shrines, we did the same to the Three Kings at Cologne, and again were greeted by a remarkable gold, Gothic, bejewelled reliquary. The Lutheran Reformation in Germany on the whole was far less iconoclastic and destructive than the Reformations in Tudor England, let alone sixteenth-century Scotland; and as a result far more medieval art survived than in Britain, in both Protestant and Catholic states. All the major buildings had already been admirably restored and reconstructed after the Anglo-American bombs, even if the street fabric of most places was all blandly new, looking a bit like Harlow New Town or Stevenage. A rare exception was Limburg-an-der-Lahn where the Hansel and Gretel half-timbered houses survived, clutching the sides of the rock on which reared the spired Gothic silhouette of the cathedral, the whole embraced in a loop of the river; it looked like a painted fantasy of the Middle Ages by Schinkel or Caspar David Friedrich; all it needed was a sprinkling of parti-coloured troubadours. The streets were full of shops selling scrumptious cakes, gingerbread and delicious plum tarts which were nearly as enjoyable as the buildings, but easier to consume.

The German Baroque palaces and gardens were the most exciting places for me. At Bruschal, the stupendous stucco, gold and scagliola imperial staircase by Balthazar Neumann had just been restored after war damage and was a dazzling mirage of fresh gilding and gleaming 'scag', in bright pistachio colours, such as real marble could hardly aspire to. The park at Schwetzingen near Mannheim, where Neoclassical garden structures had been added in the 1770s and 1780s to a Baroque layout for the Elector Palatine, included a pink Turkish mosque designed by Nicolas de Pigage (a pupil of J. F. Blondel in Paris), and was comparable to Kew, Stowe or Stourhead.

My favourite German house was Faisanerie outside Fulda: a vast place, yet unpretentious in a simple, grassy setting, rather like a Baroque version of Knole, with ochre-washed stucco ranges round courtyards and onion-domed towers. Inside were the dynastic treasures of the Hesse family – classical sculpture, eighteenth-century porcelain, paintings and furniture, much of it rescued from their houses in the Communist East and newly arranged with taste and style by Prince Philip of Hesse. Some of the rooms had English furniture and things, reflecting the close historical relations between the Princes of Hesse and the British royal family. Less magical was the former Residenz in Fulda itself which was now the town hall and over-restored, with piped *Eine Kleine Nacht* Muzak belting out of every fireplace.

Completely hooked on the buildings of the Asam and Zimmermann brothers and Balthazar Neumann, we decided to make an unscheduled detour from Stuttgart – where we witnessed Grundig's extravagant birthday firework display the like of which I have not seen before or since – to Würzburg to see the former Prince-Bishop's Rezidenz with its Tiepolo (1752) frescoes of the Four Continents, and the Emperor Barbarossa, the only other person I encountered in Germany with red hair. It was distressing in the extreme to find that Würzburg of all places had been smashed to bits by Anglo-American bombs twenty-four years earlier in February 1945. Why Würzburg, a small episcopal capital with one of the grandest of all Baroque palaces, and a supreme treasure of European civilization? Palace, churches, streets and squares, the historic

Scots College and all its archives had been pointlessly incinerated. At least Dresden, the major railway junction of Eastern Europe, was a legitimate military target (though the huge railway station was, of course, missed entirely, and the historic core flattened instead). It was difficult to look at anything in Würzburg without a feeling of blazing shame and rage. The Germans, who have *always* shown a much deeper respect for their architectural culture than the brutish British, were doing their best to put things together again and had re-roofed the Rezidenz. Thanks to the excellent, sturdy masonry of the vaulted ceilings over the staircase and Kaisar Saal, and the intervention of an educated American officer, the Tiepolo frescoes – the climax of European Rococo art – had miraculously survived with only slight damage, now restored. The chapel, with golden Corinthian capitals and Solomonic columns, had also been totally reconstructed down to the last lapis lazuli splinter, but the rest of the palace was an empty shell, and all the *Empire* state rooms decorated in the manner of Percier et Fontaine for Jerome Bonaparte as Viceroy of Westphalia, were gone forever. The unique Baroque crane by the river had survived, and the cathedral and myriad churches were at least partly restored.

We stayed in the youth hostel in Würzburg, remembering to fold our blankets properly after the Rhineland experience. It turned out to be none other than the former women's prison, designed by an architect called Speth and illustrated by Pevsner. It has one of the most extraordinary Neo-classical façades in Europe, a powerful example of *architecture parlante*. The channelled, rusticated design comprises a large segmental arch, and above it a carved lion's head with a stone ring in its mouth like a giant door-knocker. I was thrilled to be able to say that I had stayed in this strange building, although not myself a female convict at the time.

The *Schlosses* in the surrounding country also beckoned. At Viertzhochheim, just outside Würzburg, we found a small summer palace of the bishops, with an enchanting Rococo garden full of the water jokes beloved by eighteenth-century prelates and noblemen who thought it hilarious drenching their guests with concealed jets from the vaults of grottoes or the floors of pavilions. The Bishop responsible for building the Würzburg Residenz was a nephew of the Schönborn family whose principal seat, Pommersfelden, still belonged to them and was open to the public, so we also went to see that and admire the mirror and shell encrusted grotto, the imperial staircase by Johann Dientzenhofer, and the densely hung collection of *Seicento* Italian paintings in the faded state rooms which reminded me of those at Burghley, seen on one of my English house and church perambulations during school holidays. Pommersfelden had a slightly neglected feel, as the Schönborns lived mainly in Portugal at that time, and if I were honest with myself I was a teeny bit disappointed by it. It looks better in photographs. But I am glad we went to visit it then; it saves the effort of ever going back again.

The gallant little Mini drew much admiration from the Germans along the way: they were pleasingly fascinated by this contemporary and surprisingly enterprising product of the collapsing, strike-torn British motor industry. In garages appreciative mechanics would gather round, peer into the engine and talk professionally about the 'Landkreuser'. It, like all Mini cars, had one bad design defect, in that the water in the radiator always overheated when speeding on Autobahns. Minis were constructed for more sedate urban driving. This was a bore as it meant we had to stop regularly to let the engine cool down. Sometimes more serious things went wrong. On one desperate occasion a new part was required but the German mechanics said it would have to be ordered from England and (British industrial efficiency being what it was) would take a month to arrive. I was in despair. This meant we would have to give up altogether, or tuck in our sails and hitch hike. The more remote monasteries would be inaccessible. We had piled out of the car and were hanging disconsolate around on the tarmac as the chief mechanic shook his head and made discouraging German comments, while the apprentices all nodded in agreement – rather like a tutorial at university. I was sitting on a box I had removed from the boot, wistfully studying guides and maps. I suddenly realized that the box was the tool-kit which my kind, considerate, practically-minded father had put together for us at the start, like a mechanical version of a Fortnum's picnic hamper. I had forgotten about it and never looked inside. I leapt up, lifted the lid, called the mechanics and we inspected the contents. There amidst an impressive array of wrenches, screwdrivers, spanners, pincers and coils of wire, were spare plugs, valves, thingummies and... The German apprentices pounced with glee: 'Zat eez eet.' Ten minutes later we were chugging in the Landkreuser at 80 mph back along the Autobahn away from the industrial belt, in the direction of the Arch-Abbey of Beuron, crossing the watershed from the Rhine to the Danube, and the beginning of the beautiful, rural, Catholic, imperial South.

Beuron occupies an Arcadian spot in the limestone valley of the fledgling Danube close to the Black Forest and the Bodensee. Originally founded in 777 it had been one of the most important Augustinian houses in Germany in the Middle Ages but was suppressed in the early nineteenth century. The buildings and lands had passed to the Hohenzollern Sigmaringen family. In 1863 Princess Katherina of Hohenzollern gave it to the Benedictines. Under Abbot Maurus Wolter it became the largest and most influential Benedictine abbey in Germany, a powerhouse of scholarship and art with a respected faculty of biblical studies and philosophy, a pioneering centre of Gregorian Chant, a publishing house and bindery, and its own original artistic style including architecture mosaics, fresco painting, sculpture, carving and gold and silver work. In addition to the standard Baroque eighteenth-century church and monastic ranges, Beuron was especially fascinating for its late-nineteenth-century buildings and decorations including many side chapels in the church, and the monastery library.

The School of Art had been founded by Peter Lenz, a German Nazarene whose intention was to create a new religious style for architecture and art with specific spiritual qualities, including symbolic numerical proportions derived from the ancient Middle East, and forms influenced by the early-Christian paintings and

[136]

The Arch-Abbey of Beuron

mosaics in Rome. The style spread throughout Europe, even to Monte Cassino itself where much work was carried out by the Beuron designers in the late-nineteenth century, and, as has been seen, to distant Fort Augustus in Scotland. The success of the movement was sealed by the publication in France of *l'Aesthétique de Beuron* by Paul Sérusier and Maurice Denis in 1904.

In the 1960s Beuron still had its own sculpture studios and metal workshops. It provided training in Gregorian Chant, its libraries, archives, book production and other departments were all 'admirable', and we were fascinated by all we saw there. As impressive as the mass of buildings themselves, standing on a gigantic arcaded terrace and with box edged and planted formal courtyards, an onion-topped bell tower and shapely Baroque gables, was the surrounding landscape of limestone crags and woods, a paradise of wild flowers and song birds; which so much enhanced the beauty of walks along the Danube or in the hills.

The whole Beuron experience seemed to me to be a version of

the Latin Christian Church, worth having. Here was real Western religion, something spiritual, scholarly, aesthetically aspiring; not too embarrassing in comparison with the Orthodox, or Tibetan Buddhism, and the great religions of the East. How splendidly different from all-pervasive Post-Vatican II American-social-suburban 'religion' with its close-carpeted churches, Happy Eater hymn-sandwich liturgy, drip-dry vestments and complacent, sentimental, hand-shaking congregations. For me, of course, because of my particular upbringing, Beuron was part of the genetic DNA of my cultural make-up. I was once asked by an irritating American girl on a bus in Burgundy, 'Are you going to Taizé?' 'No! To Cluny.' This topographical exchange also neatly sums up my religious views. Taizé, if you do not know, is a soft-centred happy-clappy, easy-weezy 'religious centre' and inventor of despicable sub-musical 'chants'. Cluny, of course, is the pathetic ruin of the pre-eminent Romanesque Benedictine monastery in France and the medieval pioneer of hyper-elaborate ceremonial liturgy and 'art in the service of God'.

At Beuron, as in all the German and Austrian abbeys, we visited on our mini-Grand Tour, we were treated with kindness and hospitality by the monks. They refused to accept any payment whatever for our clean comfortable rooms. The most they would let us give was a small tip 'towards the organ restoration fund' or something like that. In the refectory we dined at the Abbot's table, where the food was invariably wholesome and the local wine always welcoming. Parts of dinner and supper were conducted in silence while one of the monks read from a book, either scripture or more general, which passed over our heads. Conversation was not a problem as invariably the *gastmeister*, who looked after us, spoke perfect English. We were shown everything we were interested in: libraries, art collections, workshops. There was never any onus on us to attend the monks' religious services. But a 'when in Rome' spirit suggested that we should go occasionally to Mass while in an abbey, and sometimes to Vespers.

From Beuron we went to see Ottobeuren, a former Imperial Free

Abbey (now a lunatic asylum or prison or something). The buildings were on a large and palatial scale, with a very fine late-Baroque church (1748–54) by J. M. Fischer, well worth a detour. Thereafter we pursued a flexible, leisurely, zig-zag across country, stopping to look every time we saw an onion-topped tower, a colour-washed village or small town. We saw the abbey church at Zwiefalten where the palm tree confessionals won top prize in the exotic sins competition, and the famous Rococo pilgrimage churches such as Wies, Steinhausen and Vierzenheiligen, with their effortless froth of stucco, gilding and ingenious geometric plans. They are all masterpieces and lived up to my expectations as the architectural equivalent of the music of Haydn or Mozart. But even the unknown, small village churches were delightful, with elaborately carved pulpits, asymmetrical jelly-mould confessionals, gesticulating saints, windswept angels, and an overall sense of rippling, radiant happiness. No other architecture has ever been so effortlessly, effervescently joyful as Bavarian and Austrian late Baroque and Rococo. It is difficult to decide whether one wants Heaven to be like Schinkel's Potsdam or like the Zimmermann's churches. The German sun shone away day after day. Bright geraniums decorated the ochre-coloured cottages and farmhouses, with their little middens and neat stacks of firewood. Apples were ripening in the orchards, maize in wide, unhedged fields; we stole it and ate it off the cob as part of our picnic lunches.

The villagers were very friendly and welcoming. We encountered no stereotypical 'German' behaviour. When we stopped once at some sort of tavern and asked for something to eat and drink, delicious Munich beer, bread and ham were produced, and served with merriment by the middle-aged German couple. It was only afterwards that we realized the place was closed and they had done this out of kindness. How very different from our own dear homeland. It was difficult to reconcile these people with the militaristic race who in the preceding sixty years had destroyed the lives – as much of those who lived as those who had died – of one's families, neighbours and friends.

It was an Elysium – a true Garden of Eden, closer in spirit to the warm, cheerful, European South than the grey Gothic North. I was twenty going on twenty-one. For a moment, happiness almost seemed something that I might aspire to? Unflawed rays did shine through in the years ahead – especially in my first terms at Oxford, though it was not until I was over thirty, with books to write, worthwhile jobs and a certain economic independence that I knew a degree of personal satisfaction and contentment which most of us call 'happiness'; at least those of us realistic enough not to aspire to ecstasy. 'Whatever hour of good fortune God may have given you, seize it with grateful hands.'[7] I was not always happy during the first thirty years of existence. I was too emotionally mixed up. I had ginger hair. I did not shape. I was hopelessly incompetent at all the things I was forced – or aspired – to do. The uninspiring brutality of school or the insoluble problems of home life, were, in themselves, neither here nor there. Most people face something similar or worse. A steely lack of feelings, and the vicarious alternative world of books, helped me soldier through to the calmer midlands of late youth and the pre-retirement decades of forties and fifties.

We spent some time in Munich where we stopped for a bit to imbibe the Rococo and Neoclassical architecture. We probably had too much beer as well, for I cannot remember the exact details of what we got up to there. I think we stayed away from the centre in a tower-like building somewhere near Nymphenburg (the Wittelsbach Dukes of Bavaria's summer palace and where they still lived). I remember that we drove backwards and forwards to the centre. I remember the Mini being stopped by the police for going the wrong way down a dual track road. We were completely drunk, of course, but the policeman was relaxed and un-Germanic. Realizing that we were English (perhaps he could interpret the heraldry on the bumper) he told us to take more care in the future as we might kill ourselves.

While I had organized the architectural side of the tour, Andrew

7 '*Tu quamcumque Deus tibi fortunaverit horam grata sume manu*' (Horace). As Cardinal Consalvi quoted on his state entry into Rome in 1800.

MacLaren had planned various musical treats which were to cul-
minate in Vienna. In Munich we attended the opera in the handsomely restored Neoclassical theatre by Karl von Fischer (1820s)
next to the Residenz. This is not to be muddled with the Cuvilliés
Theatre (1750) within the Residenz itself, a Rococo masterpiece
and one of those few buildings, or rooms, called after its architect
or decorator, like the Cameron Gallery at Tsarskoe Selo, the
Raphael Loggia in the Vatican or the Eiffel Tower. I cannot think of
many historical English examples apart from the various ranges at
Balliol or the Webb Building at Greenwich, can you? François
Cuvilliés, who came from Brussels and trained in Paris, was a dwarf
– the only architect-dwarf. The Cuvilliés Theatre interior, being
constructed of carved and gilded wood, had been carefully dismantled and stored during the war, which was just as well, as most
of the Residenz had been gutted. By 1969 the extravagant interior
of the theatre with its caryatids and cartouches had been put back
and fully restored, but the Leo von Klenze rooms of Ludwig I were
still shells awaiting full reconstruction; nevertheless there was much
to see in this palace inspired by a love of Italy over several generations of the Wittelsbach family. This aura came through strongly
everywhere in Munich, but especially in the Residenz, and its sixteenth-century vaulted and frescoed hall with a collection of antique
busts round the walls. The newly displayed Schatzkammer or Trea-
sury was the most impressive I had ever seen, with its cups and
dishes of agate, chalcedony and carved rock crystal, and medieval
and Renaissance jewels. To my taste, it was more impressive than
the Schatzkammer in Vienna which we saw later in our tour.

Many of the prominent buildings in Munich had been reconstructed as shells with the walls repaired and new roofs, but not
then any attempt to restore the historic interiors; as in the case of
Klenze's Glyptothek which housed Ludwig I's Neoclassical collection of Greek and Roman sculpture, including the pediment from
the Temple at Aegina and the Barberini Faun. The latter was one of
the few important antique marbles to have received an export
permit from Neoclassical Rome. Ludwig's pleas to have it had been

successful, despite the opposition of Canova. It had been admired by Winckelmann and even the Marquis de Sade, who thought it sublime. Others, however, rather surprisingly considered it to be 'indecent', with its sprawling, sleeping posture and intimation of drunkenness, which may have encouraged the papal officials to let it go to Bavaria.

The then partial state of restoration of the war-damaged interiors was moving in a Piranesian way. This was true of Klenze's Roman-style Pinakothek (1822–30), where fissures in the walls had been rebuilt with plain masonry and the principal staircase, rising in two flights to the left and right, had only bare brick walls. The Ludwigstrasse, the long broad stuccoed early-nineteenth-century street leading north from the Residenz to the Propylaeum, had also been reconstructed but not yet authentically painted to represent stone, as it is now. Fortunately, the two supreme masterpieces of Rococo architecture had escaped lightly. The famous Amalienburg is an enchanting, single-storeyed pavilion in the park of Nymphenburg. It contains a circular silver and blue mirrored saloon with a dome; silver and blue being the heraldic colours of the Wittelsbachs, and Bavaria (as displayed in the BMW car badge).

The Asamkirche (St John Nepomuk), built 1733–46, could be another contender for a building named after its architect, though in this case Asam was the name of the benefactor. The architect, Egid Quirim Asam, was also the patron, paying entirely himself for the construction of this amazingly theatrical church next to his own house with direct access to his personal tribune pew at first floor level, the *piano nobile*. It is a striking demonstration of the religious piety that inspired many Bavarian and Austrian eighteenth-century artists. The interior exaggeratedly tall and narrow, on the confined street site, has undulating walls embellished with sumptuous stucco work and scagliola, and is perhaps closer to the Baroque of Rome, where the two Asam brothers had studied for some time, than the paler more pastel Rococo generally found in Bavaria.

We also went out of town to inspect a couple of Mad Ludwig II's folly palaces, Linderhof and Herrenchiemsee. The latter involved a boat trip across the lake which was romantic enough, but the place itself was an anti-climax. Herrenchiemsee was never finished and struck me as a mediocre copy of the centre of Versailles. I thought the Mad Ludwig buildings in general were disappointing 'in the flesh' though photogenic enough. They lack any true architectural quality, being uninspired in their overall design and gross in detail. I infinitely prefer Ludwig I's architecture. There is really no comparison. He was one of the greatest of all German princely patrons, and Klenze's architecture is second only to the sublime Schinkel in Prussia. It is the buildings of Klenze, Cuvilliés and the Asams which are worth crossing the world to see.

Munich was our last major stop in Germany and from there we headed off towards Austria and the next of the Benedictine monasteries on our route: Kremsmünster, which was a highlight of the journey. Situated twenty miles south of Linz, Kremsmünster is one of the leading Benedictine houses in Europe. Founded in 777, it had been subsequently enriched by Charlemagne. The buildings were gloriously reconstructed in the mid-eighteenth century to the designs of one of the supreme trinity of Austrian Baroque architects, Jakob Prandtauer. The other two were Fischer von Erlach, who designed the Karlskirche in Vienna, and Johann von Hildebrandt, designer of the Belvedere (the Viennese Blenheim for Prince Eugene of Savoy, commander-in-chief of the imperial army and Marlborough's comrade-in-arms against Louis XIV). Prandtauer, like the Asams, was a deeply religious man and much of his architectural output was ecclesiastical, including the Abbey of Melk on a crag overlooking the Danube. We visited Melk and admired the church, library and Kaiser Saal, but did not stay there as I had already decided that the less well-known and less-touristy Kremsmünster might be more interesting. I was right, for in addition to the usual facilities of the imperial Baroque monasteries intended for liturgy, learning and hospitality, Kremsmünster had several highly unusual and special features. These included a freakish Baroque skyscraper, the astonishing eight-storey-high observatory in the grounds, and the unique fish tanks – a series of beautiful colonnaded courts or cloisters with pools of water, not grass in the centre. These were (and are) stocked with fish for the monks' diet. Kremsmünster represented religion on the grand scale but with a more educational tinge than the arts and crafts of Beuron. It housed over a hundred monks, served twenty-six parishes and had a school for several hundred boys, closer in spirit to the English Benedictine abbeys with their pedagogical functions than Continental ones. The library contained 70,000 volumes, including 2,000 incunabula, and there was a strong scholarly life. The school of philosophy at Kremsmünster was widely admired, and several of the monks were 'dons' and taught at Salzburg University including the *gastmeister*, our host and friend, who lectured in English there. He gave me a copy of a learned paper in German he had published on Anglo-Saxon and Beowulf which, I am afraid, defeated my feeble attempts at translation but I still have it in my library. The Abbey also housed a fascinating museum full of armour, snuff boxes, curiosities like a chair made from the bones of the first elephant in Austria, and paintings which had been arranged by the director of the Kunsthistorisches Museum in Vienna in the nineteenth century, and not touched since, so was an atmospheric survival of historical museum display.

There was a charming Austrian, eccentric quality to the place. The staircase in the observatory was lined with portraits of young Mozart look-alikes in red coats and powdered hair – 'our old boys' – and the rooms contained fossils, minerals and scientific equipment, and horrible things in glass jars of formaldehyde – foetuses, freaks, and two-headed animals. From the top there was a memorable aerial view of the monastic buildings, including the fish tanks. Some workmen were re-roofing one range, and flinging the broken old tiles over the parapet where they smashed far below, punctuating the music of rehearsing piano students in the adjoining rooms with staccato crashes.

In Linz itself we were beneficiaries of the hospitality of some family friends of Chris Hollis. Assuming that we must have had nothing to eat for weeks during our frugal travels, these kind-hearted folk stuffed us like Périgord geese. They took us to see the tobacco factory in Linz, an International Modern building erected in 1934, as well as the former abbey church at Weltenburg, perhaps the supreme masterpiece of the Asam brothers and the most theatrical of all Austrian Baroque interiors. The buildings were situated like so many of the monasteries on the banks of the Danube, in a romantically isolated spot. The church, built between 1716 and 1721, was oval in plan, with an almost incredible set-piece high altar-scape. Above the tabernacle a larger-than-life-size silver equestrian statue of St George galloped out between a frame-work of twisted Solomonic columns to slay a large silver dragon silhouetted against a frescoed background, and the whole dramati-cally lit from concealed sources in the vaults above. We gasped aloud at this wondrous *tableau vivant*, much to the delight of our Austrian hosts. Any lingering Northern doubts about the Berni-nesque approach to art, architecture and sculpture were dissolved on the spot, and I was hooked for life by the passionate emotional-ism of Southern Baroque.

Our hosts conducted us to the gates of St Florian on 9 September and introduced us to the *gastmeister*, the monkish scion of a rich shipping family with all the characteristics which that implies. We had to converse with him in bad French. I had warned my com-panions that the Augustinian rule was 'laxer' than that of the Benedictines, but nothing had prepared us for the palatial experi-ence that awaited, redolent of the glory and pride of Austria after the defeat of the Turks. St Florian was the only one of the Baroque monastic rebuildings which had been completed on the largest scale. It formed a regular plan constructed between 1686 and 1700 round a series of large courtyards and quadrangles to the designs of Carlo Carlone and Jakob Prandtauer. The principal court was bigger than Tom Quad at Christ Church, Oxford, its lawn adorned with clipped conical yews. In the middle was a huge stone fountain with the imperial double-headed eagle. The long ochre-washed façades were punctuated in the centre of each side by a dominant architectural feature such as the Imperial Marble Hall

St Florian: the Imperial Marble Hall

The Library

or the Grand Staircase represented by rising flights of open archways.

The church was the first part to be rebuilt in 1686 to the design of Carlo Carlone, an Italian architect active in Austria. It is literally an Italian Baroque basilica, having subsequently been raised to privileged basilica status by the Pope. The twin-towered façade looks like a stray from Rome. Inside, giant Corinthian columns whooshed up to ceiling vaults covered with murals by Martin and Bartolomeo Altomonte (more Italians) and framed in stucco, gilding and huge representations of the Abbey's and the Imperial arms. The basilica of St Florian is famous for the historic organ built by F. X. Chrismann *circa* 1770, with its 7,000 pipes and on which Anton Bruckner had played. The *gastmeister* spoke of the famous nineteenth-century musician and protégé of the Abbey as if he were almost a contemporary. We were shown his tomb in the crypt, strewn with fresh flowers, and his simple rooms with a little iron bed and the piano on which he had composed the Requiem. The excellent musical tradition was maintained by the St Florian boys' choir, one of the few to survive on the Continent, and similar to the Hofburg Chapel Choir in Vienna, even wearing the same off-duty uniform of sailor-suits.

While in Munich I had been knocked over backwards by Altdorfer's *Battle of the Isthmus* in the Pinakotek, and conceived a huge admiration for this contemporary of Dürer, rarely encountered in England. I was entranced by his vast landscape distances, blue mountains, amazing sunset skies, and little elongated figures. And so everywhere we went, I asked if, by any chance, they had a picture by Altdorfer? 'Yes,' said the *gastmeister*, 'fourteen', and conducted us to the special gallery in which they hung. Altdorfer had been commissioned in 1518 to paint this large group of panels, devoted to the martyrdom of St Sebastian (patron saint of Austria), for the altarpiece of the previous church. When the church was rebuilt in the late-seventeenth century, the pictures had been carefully preserved and were in excellent condition, the largest group of paintings by the artist anywhere in the world.

Everything at St Florian was on the heroic scale and impressively maintained. The breathtakingly long corridors were made infinite by *trompe* perspectives painted on the end walls. The library contained 140,000 volumes, double the Kremsmünster count, and the room itself was magnificent with richly carved, curvaceous, cases and a ceiling frescoed in gold and blue in 1750 by Bartolomeo Altomonte. The imperial state apartment, on the second floor, as at Chatsworth, was approached through the Marble Hall, an audience hall for the reception of the Emperor. It was a blaze of scagliola and murals by Martin and Bartolomeo Altomonte showing Prince Eugene, with divine assistance, defeating the Turks at the gates of Vienna. The apartment itself comprised no fewer than thirteen rooms, larger than the King's state apartments at Versailles or Hampton Court; an enfilade of polished parquetry, Genoa velvets and Venetian glass. Our own rooms were slightly more modest.

Although September, the Summer Refectory was still in use. It was like an orangery flooded with light, from tall arched windows, and the ceiling frescoed with bright cheerful colours in a glorious eighteenth-century, pleasure-loving manner. At breakfast, hot milky coffee was served in large deep bowls, like soup dishes, and you broke your freshly baked bread into it. This would have been delicious, if I had not mistaken the eighteenth-century porcelain containers full of white granules down the centre of the table for sugar. They were salt. That got my birthday off to a good start and made me rather thirsty for the rest of the day. My friends took me out to lunch in a village tavern somewhere in the country. Bottle of wine followed bottle of wine and I got completely, gloriously, Baroquely drunk.

We stayed at one more abbey, before Vienna, Altenburg (founded in 1144), which was my favourite of the lot. It lacked the heroic grandeur of St Florian, the charming eccentricity of Kremsmünster or the nineteenth- century contribution at Beuron, but Altenburg was a stellar collection of dazzling buildings situated in a remote forest landscape. Altenburg, too, was very large – the main façade was a quarter of a mile long – but irregular; its

Altenburg

buildings arranged round no fewer than six courts of different sizes. When we were there it was being beautifully restored after occupation by the Russian army only a decade and a half earlier. Dom Leo, the Abbot, who personally looked after us, was the cheeriest and friendliest of all the monks we met. He was touchingly proud of Altenburg, and a man of unaffected simplicity. He was the clever son of the pre-war head gardener at the Abbey, had entered the community, and now after the departure of the Communists and the Benedictine restoration, had come back to his old home as Abbot. As we walked down an interminable vaulted passage we heard ting-a-ling-ling-ling and a bicycle shot past. 'Yes, we all travel round on bikes inside. The building is so vast.' When I mentioned the next day that I had lain awake listening to some animals snuffling below the windows he replied: 'The wild boar always come up to the walls at this time of year to eat the apples which have fallen on the grass in the orchard.' As well as wild boar, the gardens and orchards were also full of wild partridge, like a medieval *mille fleurs* tapestry.

The buildings had the delicious Rococo lightness of late Austrian Baroque and included, as well as a Festival Hall, two great staircases, and state apartments, three interiors of disarming beauty. The church itself was oval in plan with bright polychromy and gilding, designed by an architect called Muggernast. The library was one of the most beautiful rooms I have ever seen, with gilded bookcases, witty frescoes on the ceiling by Paul Troger, who did most of the painting at Altenburg, and absolutely stunning scagliola columns in milky shades of lapis lazuli blue or raspberry sorbet pink. The ceiling paintings included one of Moses with the tablets of stone, pointing to the Eighth Commandment: 'Thou shalt not steal.' This jocular hint to would-be book thieves had not deterred the Russians soldiery who had helped themselves to the contents of the lower shelf all the way round.

The *pièce de résistance* at Altenburg, however, was the Crypt of the Dance of Death. This was entirely frescoed with cheerfully dancing skeletons and garlands of flowers in a light, decorative vein, reminiscent of the secular *singeries* of the period. It had the feeling of a ballroom, or a *sala terrene* for summer picnics, rather than a setting for solemn Catholic obsequies. It was the quintessence of *dix-huitième* frivolity – *joie de mort*. I wondered what one of the young monks at Fort Augustus, Father Francis Davidson, would have made of it. He was no fool, having read English at Oxford and Philosophy at Freiburg, but he was not on my wavelength and was the archetypal dour, rationalist Scot. He had once entered my study at school and found me reading a book on eighteenth-century porcelain – Chelsea, Bow, Vincennes and Meissen. He picked it up, as with tongs, looked at the pictures, grimaced in the way one might when catching a chap *in flagrante delicto* with depraved pornography, and said 'I cannot tell you, boy, how much I despise this sort of thing – the worst of eighteenth-century decadence', and walked out. An encouragement? I returned, unperturbed, to my page and was soon lost in the mysteries of 'The girl in a swing' factory. I *wish* he had been with us in the Crypt of the Dance of Death at Altenburg.

We did get to Vienna in the end. The main treats there were not architectural, but musical. Andrew had booked us into the opera season (with the cheapest available student tickets) both at the Stadt Opera and the Volks Opera. The latter was largely Mozart. I remember a production of *The Magic Flute* with a pretty pantomimey set, but it was the Stadt Opera that made an unforgettable impact. Recently reopened after war damage by the Americans, who had mistaken it for the railway station and bombed it, the 1869 foyer and staircases were pure architectural theatre, all neo-Baroque marble and gold, newly glistening. The auditorium, however, was a completely modern and unadorned 1960s structure. The stage had been equipped with the most advanced mechanical facilities in Europe and was capable of impressive set changes and rearrangements. We saw several parts of Wagner's Ring – culminating in *Götterdämmerung* with a star-studded cast, including Birgit Nielson as Brünhilde. This was a special treat and one of those remarkable coincidences of time and place, as we had accidentally stumbled on the centenary season of the Stadt Opera. The end of the gods in the last act of *Götterdämmerung* was a never to be forgotten *tour de force*; the whole set erupting in fire and flood, black clouds and then the final spectacular immolation of Valhalla, with the stage collapsing and reforming in a sustained piece of new mechanical virtuosity.

We had not come prepared for the formality of life in Vienna, and though we had managed to dredge up a clean shirt or two, had to borrow ties (compulsory at the Opera) from the ticket office, even for our obscure seats remote from the dress circle.

Another musical treat was Sunday Mass at the Augustinian Kapelle attached to the Hofburg. The original Gothic of this church was much overlaid with eighteenth-century 'comfort and joy', glass chandeliers and crimson velvet *prie dieux*. Here were performed complete Mozart and Haydn Masses with professional choir and orchestra all the year round. The fashionable congregation, dressed in Euro-smart clothes, tended to wander around the aisles during the service, and to my Northern sensibilities it had more the feel of a concert than a religious occasion, though not touristy like the Hofburg Kapelle with the Vienna Boys' Choir.

The Hofburg itself, after travelling across Europe to see it, was in some respects a disappointment. It seemed dowdy compared to many of the glittery German houses and palaces which we had seen. The Emperor Franz Joseph's rooms with their simple iron bed and ugly French-polished late-nineteenth-century Maples furniture were of some historic interest for their very dreariness and as an image of Spartan, hopeless devotion to duty and tragic self-discipline. The Imperial Library by Fischer von Erlach alone seemed a Baroque masterpiece out of the top drawer. Altogether Vienna on this first visit was an architectural anticlimax for me, though I came to see its many beauties and charms later on, and today it is one of my favourite cities. Only the Belvedere and the Karlskirche got my pulse racing in 1969. An air of shabby postwar gloom and despondency still hung over everything in those years, and the proximity of the Iron Curtain did not help. It is very different today. The 'Victorian' public buildings round the Ringstrasse seemed pompous and unoriginal in their variegated styles, compared to the nineteenth-century buildings in London. They could be trumped every time by the Gothic Palace of Westminster, the Grecian British Museum, the Italianate Foreign Office, Byzantine Westminster Cathedral, or other masterpieces I was used to, or even took for granted, at home.

The trusty Mini finally gave up the ghost in Vienna, and the engine collapsed amidst general recrimination. The contents of the mechanical hamper were now exhausted and there were no more spare parts to supply the need, nor ingenious German mechanics to minister to the stricken innards. We had had enough of each other's company, too. So we bought rail tickets back to London, put the Mini on a train-trailer and returned home across Europe to Ostend in the nineteenth-century manner; stony- broke, stuffed to the gills with art, music and architecture, scruffy, irritable and exhausted; a dying fall, but it had been a good birthday outing.

8

Oxford

It was England at last in October 1970 when I matriculated at
Oxford. Cooper's marmalade for breakfast, anchovy toast for
tea, bonfires of damp autumn leaves, Floris 89, soft Cotswold land-
scapes, golden oolite stone, choral evensong in college chapels, all
came to me as a novel experience, and yet at the same time had the
recognizable feel of a comfortable well-cut suit of clothes; it was
familiar and easy-fitting even though it was new. Perhaps this was
the 'real me'? My Scottish ancestry is so attenuated that any claim
to be Scots is similar to a would-be Hibernian-American president
clutching at Celtic straws in election year. It was only the accidents
of my early education (and I would *never* have chosen that myself)
which had emphasized the Scottish aspect. After all, by heredity
and choice, I am 50% a Londoner and could not really live
anywhere else. (Sorry to reveal this inconvenient fact so late in the
story.)

Despite everything, I sometimes loved England. Apart from the
undemanding ease of living in a country which is an incompetently
run, decaying muddle, there are also positive points: the softness
and beauty of some of the people (in my opinion, only the Italians
are better looking), the swish and glitter and variety of London, the
homely eccentricity of stolid country towns where they survived.
Above all I loved the landscape, in some cases still surprisingly well-
preserved and, of course, the architecture. Oxford symbolised all
this for me; the largest concentration of secular Gothic in the world
and, if you counted in Blenheim, the finest group of English
Baroque buildings outside the capital. Looking from the windows
of the Codrington Library at All Souls towards the dome of the
Radcliffe Camera you could almost imagine yourself in a princely
Baroque abbey somewhere in the Holy Roman Empire.

Most of the leading Victorian architects were also well represented – Butterfield, Burges, Gilbert Scott, Bodley, Waterhouse,
Street, as well as the home team of the Bucklers and Anglo-Jackson.
James Wyatt's Radcliffe Camera or Cockerell's Ashmolean were
both Neoclassical masterpieces, and landmarks in the Greek
Revival. Horace Walpole thought Oxford 'one of the most agree-
able places I ever set my eyes on'. I agreed with him. The total
ensemble was harmonious and 'easy on the eye'. Though many of
the buildings I admired were the same as those which Horace
Walpole had appreciated, I saw them through a different lens. The
whole appearance of Oxford is contemporary, for it changes from
generation to generation. In the eighteenth century the old houses
were plastered over and given sash-windowed fronts. The Gothic
college buildings were classicized, and all the new buildings
flaunted the latest fashions from Baroque to Neoclassical, forming
a vision of revived Rome.

In the nineteenth century the medieval buildings were restored,
mullions and tracery reinstated wholesale, and the Georgian classical buildings smothered in ivy, creepers and vegetation, their
stonework allowed to flake and crumble, and gently moulder away.
All the new buildings were Gothic. Thus the city presented a
complete and unified romantic spectacle 'whispering the last
enchantments of the Middle Ages'.

In our time the approach was much more archaeological and
pedantically historical. The city's appearance accorded with academic, Pevsnerian, eclectic taste and was an outdoor museum of
architectural specimens of all kinds. They stood side by side; different styles and ages all given equal prominence, their appearance
meticulously 'conserved' with restored stonework and authentic
detailing. Even the cottages between the architectural set-pieces
were carefully cosseted with Civic Trust colour schemes. They were
not just infill between important buildings, but *examples* of vernacular or artisan Georgian or suburban Victorian.

Wandering around the streets of Oxford, I was struck by a new
insight. It is a fallacy to claim that keeping old buildings is

retrograde and ties society to an anachronistic or outdated environment. Old buildings have a chameleon character and change
their appearance from century to century. They are read differently
by successive generations. Old buildings are, therefore, as much a
contemporary part of the environment as are brand new buildings,
and are equally an expression of our own tastes and beliefs. The
new buildings in Oxford in the 1960s and 1970s by Leslie Martin,
Powell and Moya, Jim Stirling, the Smithsons or Ahrends Burton
and Koralek were all in the late Modern Style but were also treated
as 'specimens' alongside the historic buildings, and this accentuated
the thematic architectural approach.[8]

This hypothesis can be further illustrated by the changing reac-
tions to ruins over the last 300 years. In the eighteenth century they
were treated as picturesque features in the landscape; thus
Fountains and Rievaulx were incorporated as eye-catchers into
extensive garden layouts, turfed around and interpolated for effect
with trees. In the twentieth century they were more archaeologi-
cally presented: foundations uncovered, ivy and vegetation
removed. Any feeling of mouldering decay was obliterated, the
masonry re-pointed, wall-tops capped with concrete and the grass
mown to bowling green standards. Here was the reredorter, there
the refectory. I am sure there is much to be said for both
approaches, but personally I prefer ivy and elegiac soliloquies on
the transience of life, buildings and civilization, to an over-literal
reading of excavated jigsaw plans.

Anyway to me later twentieth-century Oxford was a kind of
English architectural nirvana, an expression of my interests and
enthusiasms. In the early '70s it was all looking its best as many of
the exteriors had been cleaned recently or totally refaced. The
façades gleamed with fresh, cut, crisp, new stone, while many of the
finest Georgian interiors had been redecorated by John Fowler or
under his influence. His sort of approach is now frowned on, but it

---

[8] Jacobsen's St Katz, the best, is independently sited in parkland, so does not fall
into this category.

had much to recommend it, combining historical knowledge with artistic flair and a good sense of colour and tone, too often lacking in later, over-researched restorations of historic interiors. At the time John Fowler was one of my heroes and I thought of working for him. He was encouraging, but sensibly advised me to stick to academe at least for the time being. He had a reputation for being difficult and overbearing but I found him kindness itself. He invited me to lunch in March 1970 and I spent the day with him at King John's Hunting Lodge, a small eighteenth- century Gothick folly in north Hampshire, which he had restored and used as his country retreat. Various films had been shot there, and he had used the proceeds to build a white clapboard New England-influenced library in the grounds, which he called his 'potting shed' and where we had drinks and went back there for tea in the afternoon. The whole place with its garden topiary, painted furniture and under-stated elegance struck me as the acme of civilized perfection. He had cooked a delicious lunch. It was only marred by an embarrass-ing *faux pas* on my part. There was a pineapple dessert (on pretty, cream-ware plates) and he handed me a bottle of kirsch. Rather than pouring a little over the fruit I sploshed some into my glass and swigged it down, and felt woozy for the rest of the afternoon.

John Fowler's work at Oxford had included the two Senior Common Rooms in the Wyatt building at Oriel, and this led to the War of the Geraniums. Fowler had coloured the walls of the smaller room in a good shade of green as a background to the massed ranks of gilt-framed engraved portraits of the Tractarian generation of Fellows – Newman *et al* – who had been Oriel's brief moment of glory in the early nineteenth century. The larger room he had decorated in a subtle Mannerist orangey-pink taken from the robe in the Vasari painting over the chimneypiece. As was his wont, Fowler had issued a stern edict that under no circumstances should *red* geraniums be placed in the window boxes outside, as they would clash with his colour scheme. The geraniums in the Common Room window boxes in future must always be white.

The bursar, of course, with the robust utilitarianism of his kind, had ignored this command. But he had not made allowance for an unlikely combination of Oriel rowers and aesthetes led by Hugh Trevor-Roper. The latter, as Regius Professor of Modern History, was attached *ex officio* to Oriel. On his appointment he had lamented his translation to the 'dingiest, dullest college in Oxford' and determined to brighten things up. He was no philistine, and appreciated style in decoration of houses etc as much as in written prose. (Once reading something I had written, he sighed and said what a pity I belonged to a post-literate generation.) His wife, Lady Xandra, was the cynosure of Taste in Oxford, and their house on the edge of Christ Church (to which one was sometimes bidden to Sunday lunch or drinks) was a by-word for elegance, and often the subject of illustrated articles in fashionable magazines. Trevor-Roper also enjoyed mischief. He had been partly responsible for Fowler's introduction to Oxford in the first place, especially for the decoration of the magnificent library at Christ Church – one of the best Fowler works. Soon after I first arrived at Oriel, I dined on High Table and sat next to Trevor-Roper at dessert in the Common Room. We spoke entirely about Georgian interiors and the work of John Fowler, and, as far as I can remember, did not touch on history at all. The red geraniums on the windowsills outside were a personal affront. A plot was hatched. At one of the rowers' cele-bratory revels – Oriel was a rowing college *par excellence* – the red geraniums all disappeared. There was a certain amount of tutting over this hearty hooliganism, but every time the red geraniums returned they met the same fate. Once the bursar took the hint, however, and white geraniums were planted in the Common Room boxes, they were left undisturbed and bloomed clash-free.

I have rattled on about the impact of the architecture – *ars longa, vita brevis* – but Oxford also meant new friends for me. I met there many soulmates for life, not just people who were at the university – though they formed the core – but others who were connected or related in some way – friends of friends, people who lived nearby, siblings of undergraduates. Even thirty years later and, despite what is probably an unusually broad social range, it is these muckers I still find the most sympathetic. Clever people who can follow the thread of conversation, perform leaps of thought, do not need 't's crossing and 'i's dotting, with a sense of humour, shared values and interests and – a particularly Oxonian trait – the ability to converse in sustained flights of irony. Though many of my closest friends and contemporaries have not, alas, made old bones.

The first person I met at Oriel, Colin McMordie, died (when working as a picture dealer in Paris) from an operation to remove his tonsils while still in his thirties. This simple routine operation, which many children used to have on the kitchen table, is apparently dangerous when perpetrated later in life, and his heart stopped of the shock. I can remember meeting him at Oriel with vivid clarity. I had gone to one of those initiatory sherry parties, and bumped into a group of art historians including John de Witt and Colin, who was describing Durham Cathedral and quoted Pevsner's description of Wyatt's rose window as 'spidery'. I knew instantly that he was a sympathetic soul and that we would get on. It turned out that he had a motor, and was interested in exploring the surrounding country. The following Saturday we went to see Waddesdon in all its Rothschild splendour: *tous les Louis* and bright macaws flying free in the trees; this was the first of many memorable joint visits to remarkable places. Colin was doing Professor Francis Haskell's one year postgraduate French art history course before embarking on a thesis devoted to Neoclassical landscape painting. A co-pupil was Rosemary Gilbert (an admiral's daughter and great-granddaughter of the sculptor of Eros at Piccadilly Circus), who also became a firm friend, and we went around that year as a threesome, before Rosemary departed to marry her naval captain fiancé. Her more down-to-earth practical approach to life balanced Colin's Irish whimsy nicely. It always amused me in the holidays to compare their postcard style. Colin's were rose-tinted raptures: golden Paris, the Neoclassical paintings in the Louvre, romantic splendour in general. Rosemary's pointed out that the hotel had no hot water, a leaking roof, and the noise in the street outside made repose impossible.

Colin McMordie

Most people meeting Colin for the first time were struck by his pre-war good looks. These were not an unmitigated blessing as he tended to rely on them too much when dealing with other people and this led to academic and professional disappointment, but from the social point of view they were conducive to success, especially with older men. Jim Lees-Milne, for instance, thought him the image of the young Desmond Guinness with blue eyes and blond hair, and always referred to him as 'beautiful Colin'. It was other aspects of Colin's personality that appealed to me: his charm and wit, the slight Irish lilt in his accent, his well-stocked mind. It was not so much his intelligence as his particular way of looking at the world that intrigued me. He was able to appreciate 'things' in the same way that I did, and to see the point immediately. In other words we were on exactly the same wavelength, and for three years he was my best friend. This type of intellectual sympathy is rare, and a blessing when it occurs. It was short-lived, as such human symbiosis nearly always is, but I valued it at the time.

Howard Colvin always gave a lunch party for his pupils at the beginning of Michaelmas term in St Giles House, once the judges' lodgings but now part of St John's. It had an unexpected stone model of the Radcliffe Camera in the back garden. At lunch there I met Gervase Jackson-Stops from Christ Church, one of the brightest architectural historians of his generation, later the historic buildings advisor to the National Trust and organizer of the Treasure Houses Exhibition in Washington. His principal achievement in those years, though, was the rescue and resuscitation of the menagerie at Horton in Northamptonshire, an eighteenth-century Rococo folly designed by 'Wizard' Wright, which Gervase saved from ruin and restored for his own occupation.

He became a key figure in what in the late 1970s and early 1980s was christened the 'National Trust Navy'. It was an architectural/aesthete offshoot of the 'Young Fogey' movement and already a historical footnote. In Gervase's case, a charming stuttering manner concealed an unflinching determination to get things done, and at the National Trust he was responsible for many of the

achievements of the 1980s. He played an important role in saving
the landscape garden at Stowe, where the restored Chinese pavilion is a memorial to him, and he was responsible for the Trust
taking on Canons Ashby, the romantic decaying Northamptonshire
seat of the Drydens, and cajoling private benefactors to put up the
money for buying back the original furniture. Gervase, like Colin,
died comparatively young, tragically from Aids.

While in obituary mode, I will refer here to the late Glynn Boyd
Harte, from the Royal College of Art, though he was not himself at
Oxford. He became part of our circle and seems in retrospect an
essential part of the fun, visiting often and drawing astonishing
portraits – caricatures, we hoped – with multi-coloured pencils of
various local luminaries including Lady Xandra and Jeremy Catto
(History Fellow of Oriel), as well as of me, some of which were
included in due course in his first one-man exhibition at the Thumb
Gallery in Soho in 1976 (its catalogue prefaced by Tom Stoppard).
Later Glynn moved on to his real artistic métier: still-lives and
architectural paintings. His wide architectural tastes were always a
strong bond between us. Colin met the GBHs first. He came back
after Easter from Venice, and said 'I have just made friends with
these amusing artists, Glynn and Carrie, they were on their honey-
moon, staying in the same *pensione* behind the Salute, and have
asked us to supper in their new house in Cloudesley Square.' So off
we went to Islington, met Glynn and Carrie in the Camden Head
pub and walked back to an uninhabitable Georgian wreck where
the builders had just started the long, slow job of repair. We
removed a bit of rusty corrugated iron from a broken window,
climbed in and ate a picnic off the floor. This room was to be their
drawing room, decorated by Glynn with painted oak graining, a
technique he revived using combs, brushes and tins of Mander's
Matzine acquired by the gallon from closing down sales in old-
fashioned paint shops. Cloudesley Square was the first of three
beautiful houses which the GBHs were to revive and inhabit over
the years, and the setting for a succession of jollifications where
people turned up dressed as cardinals or cactuses.

Such light-hearted parties were not unknown in Oriel. Bruce Wannell, the college aesthete *par excellence* (a Persian scholar and Islamist who later had musical evenings in Peshawar to keep Afghan culture alive) gave a series of extravaganzas in his rooms in the Robinson Building, including a *fête champêtre* with a real sheep which he borrowed from a farmer at Witham, and a 'Decadence Party' where we dressed up and read late-nineteenth-century poetry. It was for that occasion that I emphasized my passing resemblance to the young Swinburne by growing a little red beard and wearing a black velvet jacket, both of which I adopted as my permanent uniform for a time. Fortunately, few photographs seem to survive, so a veil can be drawn over that excruciating lapse of discretion and taste. Bruce himself was once arrested by the police for murder after he sent his port-stained dress shirt to the laundry and was mistaken for the Oxford Ripper. Generally we wore old tweed coats, pullovers or – a strange sartorial combination – the top half of a pinstripe suit with jeans, and black brogues or Gucci shoes with horse snaffles across the front. We did not care very much about clothes, which explains the background to a joke 'fashion' competition held in college as part of the celebrations organized by Robby Lyle to mark Britain's accession to the Common Market in 1973. I still have the list of winners.

Oriel was a nice, old-fashioned college in the early 1970s, with a mascot heraldic tortoise in the Front Quad and lots of societies and clubs including the Hippocrene, a drunken dining club, and the Arnold, a more respectable historical society with talks and port. The denizens of Oriel were a good mix, with hearty rowers, who had their own table in Hall where they gorged on steak and similar hunk-building food, serious scholars, historians, even a couple of future Conservative MPs – Andrew Rowbotham and Michael Trend – and a quota of glamorous, sophisticated Harrovians who struck me as wildly 'smooth', funny, decadent and druggy. I remember one eating a live goldfish under the influence. But the atmosphere on the whole was friendly and civilized. I became the president of the JCR Art Committee, an excellent body which

JMR at the Hyde Park Hotel, 1973 – the Swinburne phase

acquired paintings and etchings to lend to all college rooms on a yearly basis. This had many perks, including cascades of invitations to private views in London and Oxford from optimistic gallery owners and dealers who probably thought our budget was much more lavish than in fact it was; as well as the opportunity to acquire pictures for oneself if the rest of the Committee turned down things one had acquired 'on spec' or reserved for further consideration. Thus I bought a reduced version of Thomas Lawrence's painting of *Kemble as Rolla*, murdering his son (from Sheridan's eponymous play). Everybody else thought it horrible. Today it graces my drawing room in Lancashire.

Through another friend in college, Richard Holmes, I was also involved in running (and became president of) the Oxford University Architectural Society. We operated in conjunction with the excellent architecture department at Oxford Polytechnic (Oxford Brooks University) and arranged one evening meeting a week in the Museum of Modern Art, with lectures alternating between poly-organized Modern Architecture and a historical topic chosen by me on behalf of OUAS. Thus one week we could hear Professor Misha Black talking about 'Los Angeles and Twentieth-Century Town Planning' and the next Roderick Gradidge on Victorian pubs or Professor Joe Mordaunt Crook on William Burges. Such nine-teenth-century subjects marked my recent conversion to Victorian architecture. I had arrived at Oxford with conventional Georgian tastes, starry-eyed about John Fowler. At Oxford these prejudices dissolved and Victorian buildings, which I had sometimes previously thought hideous, suddenly seemed magnificent and among the best things ever produced in this country. This belated enlight-enment owed much to the guidance of Peter Howell, then a classics lecturer at Bedford College, London, but who had retained and still lived in a flat in North Oxford. When up at Balliol in the 1960s, Peter had led a successful undergraduate campaign to stop the College demolishing the Waterhouse hall and Broad Street range there. He was a doughty champion of all Victorian buildings and through his eyes I came to see their point, especially the supreme quality of Victorian Gothic churches: the hard geometries of Street, the glacial perfection of Pearson, the glorious polychromy of Butterfield, and the patrician refinement of Bodley.

Apart from Architecture, the other university society with which I involved myself and became president of was the Gregorian Chant Society. We sang three Latin Masses a term, in Campion Hall Chapel (Lutyens!), but had convivial rehearsals every week in different colleges – Magdalen, Exeter and Keble. Some of the members were Catholics from Benedictine schools like myself, but many of the strongest supporters were Anglicans, including Edward Bundock who is now the rector of eight medieval churches in Norfolk. I manned a stall at Freshers Fair in the Schools each year and managed to net quite a number of aficionados including Mark Studer and Nick John, who were reading Law, but not their legal confrère Tony Blair despite the fact that he had been a chorister at Durham Cathedral as a boy. He had graduated to the guitar. Nick, Mark and the other Gregorian chanters were part of a special network of non-Oriel friends at Oxford, and thereafter. Nick became dramaturge at ENO but was killed in a walking accident in Lichtenstein. He is the only one of my contemporaries to have secured a place in the *DNB*. Hugh Montgomery-Massingberd's sister Mary was a strong supporter and introduced me to Hugh. The other girls in OUGCS included beautiful, saintly Santha Bhattarjargi, from Somerville, who later became an Anglican nun, and also died young, working among the poor and sick in India.

The celebrant at our Masses was Dom James Forbes, OSB, the Master of St Benet's Hall. Father James, from Ampleforth, was the third, and the last, of the admirable Benedictine monks who had a significant influence on me in my youth: Aidan Trafford and John Lane Fox being the other two, as will be recalled. In Oxford I never attended Mass at the Catholic Chaplaincy, then in the charge of Crispian Hollis and a hotbed of hideous modernism, though I once had lunch there. I immediately made my way to St Benet's, originally Hunter Blair's Hall (with its Fort Augustan connections), and met the Master, Father James. He was a colourful pipe-smoking character, welcoming and hospitable. He was even more reactionary than myself, and a man of taste.

Affectionate but probably apocryphal stories circulated about Father James's social views. Boy in confession: 'I am afraid it concerns a lady, Father.' 'Lady *Who*?' Or returning to Ampleforth after helping out at Warrington, one of the Benedictine Lancashire parishes, and being asked if he had enjoyed it. 'Yes. Active, devoted parish. Very friendly place... But of course, *nobody* lives there!'

He looked like an *ancien régime* cleric by Largillière, and had a nice dry humour. He ran the place very well and kept it healthily in the black in the lean days after the Second Vatican Council when there was a dire shortage of monkish novices, by making up the numbers with secular undergraduates – Fitzalan Howards and de Vescis – in term time and filling the place with American Summer Schools in the vacations. He treated it like a country house: there were good paintings on the walls and decent mahogany furniture in the main rooms. On his desk was a figure of a monk made from one of John Knox's vertebrae. Hunter Bunter's spirit, one felt, would have felt at home. Father James once told me that he had been much influenced by Father Alfred Gilbey's priestly role and had tried to re-create something of the atmosphere of Fisher House, the old Catholic Chaplaincy at Cambridge, at St Benet's. Like Alfred he was keen on beagling and used to go out and bless the beagles at the beginning of the season. Something of his tone can be gathered from his intervention in a conversation about nuns: 'I think there is a great role for Little Sisters of the Rich.' When I admired the pictures and furniture, and the fine china which he collected, the response, with a glance around, was 'At least it isn't drab.'

Father James was an expert on eighteenth-century porcelain, with a boundless enthusiasm for soft paste and glazes of a 'smooth buttery texture', especially the French factories: Vincennes, Sèvres, St Cloud and the small *recherché* royal factories owned by the Comte d'Artois and Marie Antoinette. He had built up an enviable collection including an especially rare Sèvres teapot. He once told me off for picking it up with only one hand, a well-deserved rebuke as a result of which I learnt to hold 'good things' with both hands. I did wonder how, with his Benedictine vow of poverty, he had managed to acquire so many beautiful objects. I received a clue years later when Mrs Salvin at Croxdale in Durham told me, 'Oh, Father James used to marry us all, and we all knew that we were expected to give him a piece of china in return as a thank you.' He held tutorials on eighteenth-century porcelain in the Ashmolean, which were a high point of my terms. I assiduously made notes which I still possess; they are a very useful introduction to the subject and I still mug them up occasionally before showing American tourists round things. He was a tremendous encourager. Under his guidance Bernard Green from Oriel became a Benedictine and Nick Sheaff went to work with ceramics at Christie's. His crusty façade clad a generous, kindly and holy man to whom I owe more than I can say. He encouraged me to write articles on architecture and introduced me to people. In fact, he did me many good turns that governed my future career.

I had intended to write my D. Phil. thesis on George III's architect James Wyatt, but discovered that Frances Fergusson (now President of Vassar) was already doing that under Professor Ackermann at Harvard. After discussion with her, and under Howard Colvin's wise and gentle guidance, I researched James's brother Samuel instead. This turned out a good decision as Samuel was, though less prolific and various, in some ways a more interesting and representative figure about whom little was known. He was architect by appointment to the Industrial and Agricultural Revolutions, a friend of Matthew Boulton and James Watt (whose houses he designed) in Birmingham, and the author of the Albion Mill at Blackfriars, the first steam-powered flour mill in the world with pioneering, brick raft foundations. He was an engineer who patented fireproof construction, and designed harbours and lighthouses. My star discovery, set off by a clue in the Trinity House archives, was that he had been estate architect to Coke of Norfolk at Holkham, for whom he had designed about fifty model farm buildings including the Great Barn, the finest of its type and unequalled in Europe or America. Through Holkham I was introduced to Dr Hassall at the Bodleian who was also librarian to the Earl of Leicester. He went over to Holkham in the vacations to catalogue the archives and supervise access to the muniment room and library. He took me with him several times so that I could study the late-eighteenth-century accounts. I soon found records of large-scale payments to Samuel Wyatt, proving my supposition. At Holkham, Dr Hassall used to stay in the William Kent temple or the Triumphal Arch, and let me stay there too. The views were wonderful – down over the lake to the sea from the temple portico, or from the Arch for miles along the great ilex avenue to Kent's obelisk and the vast Palladian house behind. Often it was misty in the mornings and you could hear the deer coughing under the trees. I walked every inch of the park looking for Wyatt, and could find my way round now in the blackest night (if ever I needed to).

Old Lord Leicester, who was not very well, was distant but welcoming. His first remark to would-be researchers in his library was 'I hope you are not going to make socialism?' (rather a nice phrase, which I have adopted). Once reassured on that count, he was friendly. It was marvellous to sit in the library and look straight down the enfilade to the chapel at the other end of the house. Lord Leicester liked all the doors left open for this reason, though others more prone to chills were not so enthusiastic. The Lord Leicester at this time was the third for whom Dr Hassall had worked, having originally got the job in the 3rd Earl's time as a fresh young graduate before the war. He had applied for a job at the British Museum but not got it. The 3rd Earl fell out with his old librarian one day when the latter came down to dinner dressed in an eiderdown as a protest against the indoor chill. 'Unforgivable and unforgettable things were uttered' and the bibliophile walked out never to return. Naturally the BM had been asked to replace him with someone suitable. The librarian there scratched his head but then remembered the rejected Hassall and suggested him. This led to endless crossed wires, as by that time Hassall had found employment at the

Bodleian in Oxford, but Lord Leicester always thought he had come over from the British Museum for the week. Lord Leicester was in the habit of giving his young (and then rather Left-wing) librarian useful advice: 'Dear boy, remember to make sure when filling one of your livings that the chap can play cricket. The village like that.'

Dr Hassall loved his food and we used to have huge lunches while he regaled me with stories. When Queen Mary came over to Holkham from Sandringham to see the library, he had shown her some of the illuminated manuscripts in which the collection is so rich. 'And what do you do when you are not here?' the royal guest had asked. 'I work at the Bodleian Library, Ma'am.' 'I laid the foundation stone of the new building there' – pause – 'and if I had known what it was going to look like I would have done nothing of the sort!'

When Dr Hassall had first gone to Holkham, there was still a full Victorian household *in situ*. On an early visit he found crumbs on the library table and was worried they might attract mice who would eat the bindings. The nonagenarian white-bearded Earl used to get up and wander round nibbling biscuits in the night. So Hassall summoned his courage and rang for the housekeeper. This formidable personage in due course arrived. Very tentatively he explained the biscuit problem. 'In *Houses*', she replied, 'tables are the province of the Groom of the Chambers', and walked out. Hassall rang again and asked for the Groom of the Chambers. In due course this even more awe-inspiring figure arrived. Hassall politely explained the problem for the second time. With a majestic sweep of an arm, the Groom of the Chambers brushed the crumbs on to the carpet and said: 'In *Houses*, floors are not the province of the Groom of the Chambers', and left the room. Defeated, Dr Hassall got the hearth brush, gathered the crumbs, and threw them out of the window.

The upshot of these Holkham research jaunts was that Dr and Mrs Hassall asked whether I would like to lodge with them in the Manor House at Wheatley during my last year. Though out of

The Manor House, Wheatley

JMR's bedroom on left, study top right

Oxford, this was a very good arrangement, as they gave me two rooms, a bedroom over the kitchen and a study in the attic. I got a lift with him every morning, and got the bus back at night, but often spent the weekends and Sunday lunch with them and their family. Mrs Hassall – when she was not travelling in Albania or whizzing round Oxfordshire on her motorbike – was a good cook. She could be formidable. Once at Encaenia, Harold Macmillan had noticed this grey-haired old lady all alone and with condescending kindness asked if he could sit next to her in his Chancellor's finery. 'You can, if you *like*,' she replied to his surprise. Wheatley provided the much-needed tranquillity required to write my thesis, most of which I did in the attic room there looking down over the garden with its round clipped box trees and view to the slopes of Shotover Hill. I have a touch of bird in me, and like a nest high up. At home I have always lived on the top floors, with views down, and in London I have a mews flat above the garage and street.

Suddenly the terrible prospect of getting a job dawned. What should I do? There seemed to be no jobs for architectural historians. I went to the careers advice office or whatever it was called. 'You must train as an accountant,' they said. 'Think of Nicholas Goodison; interested in eighteenth-century ormolu, clocks, and Matthew Boulton – just like you, but a banker and head of the Stock Exchange or something. That's what you must do.' I must have looked unconvinced, for they added, 'or the Duke of Richmond. Nice Georgian house to look after, so he became an accountant.' I did not want to be an accountant. I did not want to make money. I wanted to do something interesting in my own field.

I decided to apply for a job myself and replied to advertisements in the paper for keepers at the British Museum, or writers for the *Victoria County History* and other historical posts. The embarrassment and irritation of (failed) interviews followed. 'Why do you want to work for us?' 'I thought it might be good for me.' 'That is not the point. It is whether you would be any good for us!' At another interview one of the inquisitors said to me, with a sudden, disconcerting, direct glance: 'Of course, you have had a very privileged life?' I was so surprised, and angry, I could not respond. Privileged? What could he know about my childhood on a remote farm, about my terrible school, or my impoverished upbringing? Only a fraction of what I had encountered had caused Roy Jenkins to close down the whole English borstal system for ever, amidst a welter of liberal wailing. Privileged? The only printable response is: 'Things are very much more complex than that. And if your definition is what I think it might be, the answer is "No".'

Postscript

I spent the autumn of 1973 on the dole in London. As a result of my holiday jobs I had paid some stamps, or something, and was thus entitled to sign on as unemployed; so I queued once a week with the best at Rochester Row Labour Exchange. I borrowed a flat in Mortimer Street, the site of the sculptor Nollekens's old house on the north edge of Soho, from Brian Pilkington via the good offices of another Oxford friend, Christopher Brown (today director of the Ashmolean Museum). In the event, the prospect of interesting jobs – more interesting than accountancy – materialized. John Harris proferred me a niche at the RIBA Drawings Collection in Portman Square. This would have been a friendly, exciting experience, but pay hardly featured. John Saks, a trustee of the Morgan Library in New York, whom I had met in England, suggested that I might like to go there to catalogue their large holdings of heraldic bookplates. This was part-time and might have been a mythological doom, like pushing a rock eternally uphill. More seriously, John Cornforth, the architectural editor of *Country Life*, was looking for a new staff writer to help with the weekly country house articles. He asked me to write two trial pieces and suggested the Wyatts, developing the subject of my Oxford thesis. I worked on those while staying in Mortimer Street, and they came out in December 1973, the first of my regular contributions to *Country Life* which have continued for over thirty years. At the same time I was interviewed for a job in the GLC Historic Buildings Division. This admirable organization (destroyed by Mrs Thatcher in 1986) had been started by C. R. Ashbee in the 1890s and was responsible for the *Survey of London*, the official history of London's architecture, and day-to-day control of all listed buildings in London with the authority to direct local council planning committees, in fact

absolute power to achieve a public good. It also looked after the
GLC's own historic properties including Kenwood, Marble Hill,
and the Ranger's House at Greenwich. It was entirely a professional
body and was part of the GLC Architects' Department. It was run
by a proper architect, Ashley Barker, who had trained at the Architectural Association. It employed a mix of architects, surveyors and
historians – a proper 'multi-disciplinary team' – and was therefore
entirely free of the sclerotic bureaucracy and 'management' which
bloat and hamstring contemporary organizations like English
Heritage and the National Trust. The HB Division got on with the
practical work for which it existed, namely protecting, recording
and restoring London's historical architecture, blissfully unhin-
dered. It was remarkably successful, and almost single-handedly
halted the 1960s destruction of London with a succession of
triumphant defeats of the philistines at public inquiry. It stopped
the Leslie Martin plan for flattening Whitehall, British Rail's
proposed demolition of St Pancras Station, and various private
landlords' redevelopment schemes for Sackville Street, off
Piccadilly, the west side of Berkeley Square in Mayfair and Russell
Square in Bloomsbury. It played a key role in the resuscitation of
whole areas like Covent Garden and Spitalfields. It is one of the
reasons why today London is so much more beautiful and prosper-
ous than most English provincial towns and cities.

This seemed to me what I wanted to do. I did not just wish to be
a historian and writer. I was a campaigner. I wanted to save buildings. I wanted to fight in the front line, not retreat to an academic
ivory tower. I asked Howard Colvin for advice as to which full-time
job I should take, *Country Life* or the GLC. He recommended the
latter, as 'You never know with magazines, they can be taken over
and closed down. A public organization like the GLC Historic
Buildings Division has an assured long-term future.' So I took the
GLC's offer and started work with them at the end of January
1974, moving permanently to London and beginning a twelve-year
stint which was to be the most rewarding, effective and positive
decade in my life. Not only was the work satisfying and exciting at

the time, but I can today walk round London and take pride in what we achieved then. As for the 'assured long-term future', we were so busy saving buildings from demolition that it came as a surprise when we were demolished ourselves.